HAVEN IN THE HEART OF THE CITY

HAVEN IN THE HEART OF THE CITY

The History of

LAKEWOOD CEMETERY

LAKEWOOD CEMETERY

MINNEAPOLIS, MINNESOTA

EPITAPHS

Epitaphs add glimpses of individual lives to cemetery grandeur. They reveal the grief of parents at a child's death, the poignancy of lost love, the release of the aged when they are finally at rest.

There are thousands of epitaphs at Lakewood Cemetery. A few, marked by the symbol ❧, are included in this book.

Library of Congress Catalog Card Number: 92-85299

Copyright 1992 by Lakewood Cemetery.

All rights reserved. Except for brief quotations in a review, no part of this book may be reproduced in any manner without written permission. For information, contact Lakewood Cemetery, 3600 Hennepin Avenue South, Minneapolis, Minnesota 55408.

ISBN: 0-9635227-0-1

Research, writing, design, and production by Yeager Pine & Mundale, Minneapolis, Minnesota.

Editor and Project Director: Susan Mundale

Research and Writing: Mame Osteen

Project Manager: Bonnie Anderson

Design and Art Direction: Rachel Fine

Macintosh Layout: Stuart Job

CONTENTS

FOREWORD

The community leaders of early Minneapolis had a vision: to offer the city's families and individuals the opportunity for proper burial in a beautiful, peaceful environment. Their gift to succeeding generations is Lakewood Cemetery, truly a haven in the heart of the city.

In its early years over a century ago, many families made regular visits to Lakewood's park-like setting, often spending an entire afternoon or even a day paying respects to loved ones, enjoying the grounds, and strolling among the monuments.

Over the years, Lakewood's boundaries have been defined by fences and gates, which many residents of the city enter on only a handful of occasions throughout their lives. For most, Lakewood is a glimpse of apple blossoms in spring or monuments surrounded by brilliant maple trees in the fall. Yet Lakewood maintains its welcome to regular and occasional visitors alike. And when a loved one dies and friends or family members choose Lakewood for interment, the value of Lakewood to the city is reaffirmed.

The board of trustees has created this book as a means of sharing Lakewood's beauty with those who know it intimately, and perhaps encouraging those who only pass by to come in through the gates and see it first-hand. Equally important, in commissioning this book the trustees are honoring Lakewood's staff, past and present, who have cared for Lakewood with love and dedication.

We also honor previous trustees, who through the years have managed Lakewood's resources so responsibly. Because of their wisdom and prudent management, the families who choose Lakewood can be assured of care for the rest of time. This is the legacy of those who have been responsible for Lakewood in the past, and it is the legacy that current trustees will pass to succeeding generations.

For that reason, I would like to add a word of personal recognition of the trustees, pictured on page 116, who serve Lakewood as this is written. Their support and thoughtful deliberation on Lakewood matters has been invaluable. Also worthy of special mention are three individuals who have served in ways that perhaps only this writer can fully appreciate: my predecessor, the late John Pillsbury Snyder, Jr., president of Lakewood Cemetery Association from 1974 to 1983; David Hatlestad, Lakewood's chief operating officer from 1972 to 1989; and Ron Gjerde, Jr., our president today, an energetic, extremely capable man whose management ability is helping assure a future for Lakewood as illustrious as its past. All of these individuals exemplify the quality of service that makes Lakewood the exceptional institution we are proud to present in this book.

Henry S. Kingman, Jr.
Chairman, Board of Trustees
December 1992

Henry S. Kingman, Jr.

7

"To every thing there is a season, and a time to every purpose
under the heaven: A time to be born and a time to die."

Ecclesiastes 3:1

Evolution of the American Cemetery

Human beings, unlike other living creatures, possess the unique ability to number their days, to be aware of death as the inevitable end of individual existence.

Despite our recognition of mortality, death and dying remain shrouded in mystery: Why must we die? What does it mean? Is death a finality or merely a separation of the spirit from its earthly remains? Attempts to answer these eternal questions have contributed to the culture of every human society regardless of race, religion, or geographic origin. Myriad qualities differentiate the world's cultures, yet the distinctly human need to attribute meaning to life generates one similarity among them all: the universal desire to pay tribute to the dead with honorific rituals.

"[We] have never been able to study humans seriously without considering the essential fact of their mortality," said anthropologist Clifford Geertz in his 1973 book, *Interpretation of Cultures*. "This is because death and its rituals not only reflect social values, but are an important force in shaping them."

SHE GAVE HER LIFE TRYING TO
RESCUE HER TWO ONLY CHILDREN.

     Eva L. Mackenzie – 1865-1891

Natural beauty and quiet serenity give Lakewood Cemetery, in the city of Minneapolis, a timeless quality.

Close examination of these rituals gives observers a deeper understanding of the social life of ancient peoples. Archaeologist Richard Leakey recounts the discovery of the 60,000-year-old remains of a man found in the highlands of the Zagros Mountains in Iraq. "It would appear that the man's family, friends, and perhaps members of his tribe had gone into the fields and brought back bunches of yarrow, cornflowers, St. Barnaby's thistle, groundsel, grape hyacinths, woody horsetail, and a kind of mallow," Leakey wrote. The flowers were deliberately placed around the body of "Shanidar Man," whose remains were laid on a rough bed of woven horsetails.

In Egypt, the three great pyramids at Giza have stood in the Valley of the Nile for nearly five thousand years as monuments to the dead pharaohs buried within them. The largest monument covers 13 acres at the base and rises 482 feet into the air, the height of a 48-story building. Filled with riches, these tombs are a testament to the omnipotent power of the pharaohs, to the significance of the funeral ritual, and to the importance of creating a place of lasting significance for the dead.

SACRED BURIAL

Research has shown that despite the diversity of their rituals, most societies bury their dead in a sacred place. In the Western world, setting aside a space for interment — the burial ground, churchyard, graveyard, or cemetery — has been the norm.

Until the early 19th century, most Europeans were either buried inside or in close proximity to a church. The finest burial sites, those reserved for the rich and powerful and the clergy, were the crypts found beneath the floor of the church and close to the altar. The practice of burying royalty and influential figures within the confines of London's Westminster Abbey may seem a curiosity to us, but the tradition was routinely practiced in churches great and small throughout Europe into the 1800s, and it continues today. Just as Queen Elizabeth I, Mary, Queen of Scots, and Sir Isaac Newton lie within the confines of Westminster Abbey, so do the remains of Francis Cardinal Spellman and Bishop Fulton J. Sheen rest in tombs in New York's St. Patrick's Cathedral. Of course, the space available in churches was inadequate to serve the needs of a growing population and in time the use of adjacent graveyards developed.

Rural cemeteries were once popular recreational sites for visitors, who enjoyed the lovely park-like setting. Here, a family visits a grave at Lakewood Cemetery in 1890.

In America, the church and its nearby graveyard were central to small-town and rural life. Buried among the living, the dead remained a constant reminder of the future.

CEMETERY REFORM

By the mid-18th century, churchyards in major European cities were filled with tombstones, and the growing populations of both the living and the dead made problems unavoidable. Sacred and time-honored burial traditions were at odds with a growing, changing urban culture. The public's health consciousness, offended by the overcrowded churchyards, soon prompted written condemnation of shallow graves. The need for improved sanitation and the concern for public health were topics discussed at great length by reformers.

The public's evolving desire for urban sanitation was rooted in fundamental changes in Europe's social fabric during the 18th century, says architectural historian Richard A. Etlin. In France, the Age of Enlightenment brought with it a call for order in society, which led to the birth of modern social institutions. At the same time, Great Britain embarked on a scientific and industrial age. The demand for burial reform was one among many basic changes in society and, as such, was debated furiously in essays, letters, pamphlets, and magazines. Politicians, patricians, even poets joined the fray. In 1810, the great romantic poet William Wordsworth wrote *Essays upon Epitaphs*, in which he argued for reform.

In developing a new concept for the cemetery, British and French sensibilities merged in the construction of a tomb for the French philosopher Jean-Jacques Rousseau. Built by the Marquis de Giradin on his estate at Ermenonville in the 1770s, the tomb rested on a small artificial island shaded by poplar trees. The tranquil setting, modeled after a proper English garden, drew hundreds of visitors who experienced the association of death with peace, serenity, and nature.

Unlike the churchyards of old, nature dominates the expansive grounds of Lakewood Cemetery.

Despite heated debate, the idea of merging death with nature remained an abstraction, discussed only by the intellectuals of the day. Still, Rousseau's tomb hinted at the future.

GOVERNOR JOHN SARGENT PILLSBURY (1829-1901)

The first of his notable family to move to Minnesota, Governor John S. Pillsbury was a native of Merrimac County, New Hampshire, where he was born July 29, 1829. His father was a carpenter, hotel keeper, and farmer. Son John received a common school education and learned the painting (some say printing) trade before taking a job clerking in his brother George's country store at age 16. ■ In 1855, Pillsbury decided to move west and undertook the long and difficult trip to Minnesota's Northwest Territory. He took the train to the end of the line, Rock Island, Illinois, some 700 miles away. From there he continued northwest on a steamboat to St. Paul, and finally arrived in St. Anthony by stagecoach. He started a hardware business that, in its early years, miraculously survived both the Panic of 1857 and an enormous town fire that destroyed most of the adjacent buildings on Main Street. ■ By 1860, Pillsbury was active in politics, first serving as a St. Anthony alderman, then a state senator, before being elected governor in 1875, a position he held for three terms. ■ Also in the 1860s, Pillsbury became a champion of the University of Minnesota. He donated land, financial assistance, and a great deal of time and energy to its birth and development. He was an enthusiastic supporter of coeducation, a revolutionary idea at the time. For his service, he was appointed one of the University's first regents, a position he held for 38 years. ■ Though Pillsbury retained his hardware business until he was elected governor in 1875, he invested in a small milling operation with his nephew Charles, who joined him in St. Anthony in 1869. That business formed the foundation of a giant consumer foods industry that still bears the family name. ■ The striking Pillsbury monument, which vies with the Rocheleau monument as the tallest in Lakewood Cemetery, features a woman draped in Grecian robes standing atop a pedestal. The monument is also carved with a sheaf of wheat, symbolizing the family's milling interests.

Situated among towering oaks, the Pillsbury monument is an inspiring tribute to one of Minneapolis's most accomplished families.

Lakewood Cemetery was modeled after rural cemeteries introduced in 19th century France. When Lakewood was established in 1871, these spacious cemeteries were flourishing in the United States. Set between Lakes Calhoun and Harriet, Lakewood is considered one of the most beautiful cemeteries in the country.

PERE-LACHAISE

Early in the 19th century, the Prefect of the Seine, Nicholas Frochot, inspired by an evolving concept of death, ended a thousand years of tradition when he acquired a large estate on the outskirts of Paris. There he developed Père-Lachaise, Europe's first modern cemetery. An alternative to interment inside or adjacent to parish churches, Frochot's cemetery invoked the Greco-Roman tradition of burying the dead outside the city, a practice shared by other societies of the time, including the Chinese, the Turks, and native Americans. The timing was right, and the new cemetery became an immediate success, listed among the noteworthy sights of Paris.

Originally 48 acres and later expanded to 107, Père-Lachaise was beautifully situated. Meadows, winding roads, and forests offered visitors lovely views of nature and, from its hilltops, a panorama of the city. As its reputation spread, Père-Lachaise became the model for cemeteries throughout the world.

A CHANGING IMAGE OF DEATH

Between the 13th and the 17th centuries, grim depictions of corpses and skeletons were the predominant images of death on European tombs. In Paris, a 16th century alabaster statue of a desiccated corpse once presided over the Cemetery of the Holy Innocents, which until modern times was the largest burial ground in Europe.

In the United States, the association of death with the grotesque found similar expression in the Puritan cemeteries of 17th and 18th century New England. There, tombstone carvings —skull and crossbones, a solemn epitaph —reminded the living of their inevitable fate.

The first cemetery in the United States that embodied society's changing attitude toward death was Grove Street Cemetery, established in New Haven, Connecticut, in 1796. Occupying six acres, Grove Street was America's first private, non-denominational cemetery. People thought it was enormous, though compared to the cemeteries that followed, it was quite small. Its location, removed from the center of town, reflected the public's growing health consciousness. However, this New Burying Ground, as it was called by New Haven's citizens, was filled with stark images of death like those in the old burying grounds it replaced. Later burial monuments bore images of angels, which next to the depictions of bones and corpses, left the two visions in sharp contrast.

Removing the dead from the realm of the living, reformers succeeded not only in promoting public health but also in shifting from traditional images of decay. By interring the dead amid natural pastoral beauty, reformers established the graveyard as a place for contemplation, meditation, and commemoration.

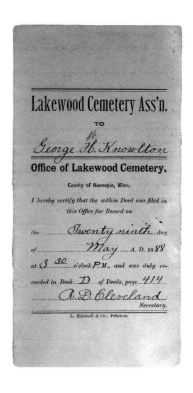

In 1888, George H. Knowlton purchased a five-grave lot in Lakewood Cemetery for $50. In exchange, he received a deed, signed by Superintendent R. D. Cleveland.

WHERE YOU ARE NOW, SO ONCE WAS I. WHERE I AM NOW, SO YOU WILL BE.

❧ 18TH CENTURY EPITAPH

THE CEMETERY IN 19TH CENTURY AMERICA

The "garden" or "rural" cemetery movement originated in 1831 with Mount Auburn Cemetery in Cambridge, Massachusetts. The first truly rural cemetery in the United States, Mount Auburn rejected the notions of the Puritan settlers who regarded the land outside Boston as a "heidious and desolate wilderness ful of wilde beasts and savage men."

WHEN THE SUN

OF BLISS IS BEAMING

LIGHT AND LOVE

UPON MY WAY,

FROM THE CROSS

THE RADIANCE STREAMING

ADDS MORE LUSTRE

TO THE DAY.

      ❰ BOWRING – 1825

         THE GARDEN OF THE

         RADIANT CROSS

         SECTION 59

Concern for public health prompted Dr. Jacob Bigelow, a physician, Harvard College professor, and civic leader, to search for an alternative to Boston's overcrowded churchyards. Bigelow was a medical botanist who had conducted the first systematic study of the region's flora. He was also widely traveled and well versed in European society. The concept of Père-Lachaise appealed to him. With partner Henry A. S. Dearborn, first president of the Massachusetts Horticultural Society and a retired army general and civil engineer, Bigelow located a 72-acre plot near the Charles River in 1829. To raise the $6,000 purchase price, Bigelow and Dearborn sold 100 charter memberships for $60 each — including one to the Horticulture Society, which planned to build an arboretum on the site.

More than 2,000 people attended Mount Auburn's dedication ceremony on September 24, 1831. U.S. Supreme Court Justice Joseph Story announced that the cemetery was destined to become an American cultural institution, an outdoor school of history and philosophy that would "preach lessons to which none may refuse to listen and which all that live must hear."

Bigelow conceived Mount Auburn's romantic landscape as "a well-managed park…[with the] grace and luxuriance of growth which good taste demands." By 1835, Mount Auburn contained 1,300 ornamental shrubs, fruit trees, and rare plants from as far away as Turkey, Italy, and India.

Mount Auburn soon became a popular recreational spot for visitors and residents of the area, who strolled the paths, picnicked on the grounds, and admired the sculptured monuments. Other cities followed Boston's example, building spacious rural cemeteries in spectacular surroundings, like Laurel Hill in Philadelphia, Green-Wood in Brooklyn, and Spring Grove in Cincinnati.

A RADICAL APPROACH

In 1844, Cincinnati established what many have called the most beautiful of all cemeteries — Spring Grove. Designed originally by Howard Daniels, who modeled it after Mount Auburn, Green-Wood, and Laurel Hill, Spring Grove took a radical approach to the landscape ideal by developing the "lawn plan" of Prussian-born gardener Adolph Strauch. The Spring Grove lawn plan defined a completely open and uncluttered space in which the beauty of nature took precedence over everything, including the burial monuments. At Spring Grove there were no hedges or fences surrounding individual graves as there were in New England cemeteries. Roads followed the natural contours of the land. Lots were large, but small, low-maintenance headstones were encouraged. Strauch's radical plan incited strong reactions from Cincinnati's residents. He received death threats after numerous articles in local newspapers condemned his plan. But criticism eventually subsided and the cemetery earned worldwide acclaim.

MANY HOPES LIE BURIED HERE. ❧ MARY STEVENS – AGE 18, JULY 27, 1867

THE VICTORIAN IDEAL

In retrospect, the birth of the "cemetery," a place of rest and repose, was the logical development of 19th century Victorian culture. Increasing urbanization and industrialization and the dramatic social changes they unleashed undermined the bleak severity of Puritan attitudes and created a new society increasingly isolated from nature. Developments in technology, science, medicine, and political thought infused citizens with optimism and a belief in progress.

In 19th century Minneapolis, Lakewood Cemetery offered visitors a rare opportunity to see fine sculpture and architecture.

These attitudes were accompanied by a growing need for commemoration among Americans who, for the first time, were developing a sense of their nation's history. Pride in a shared community life and a collective identity found expression in new American institutions. Architects created superb museums, churches, public libraries, and state capitols. Sculptors paid tribute to American events and heroes. In 1885, the Washington Monument was completed and the following year the Statue of Liberty was dedicated in New York harbor.

The cemeteries of that time had become institutions that commemorated the great leaders and events of the day. The nation's most respected architects — Richard Morris Hunt, Louis Sullivan, and Stanford White — and its prominent sculptors, including Lorado Taft and Daniel Chester French, all designed cemetery buildings and monuments. Government and civic leaders spoke eloquently of the cemetery as a place for inspiration, reflection, and contemplation.

Because of the changes in the thinking and design of the 19th century cemetery, "burial ceased to be...an insistent reminder of the brevity of life and the certainty of death," observes architectural historian Richard Etlin, and became instead "an institution of remembrance."

The Lakewood Chapel, constructed in 1910, added cremation facilities as an alternative to traditional burial. In 1920, flowers filled the chapel's crematory room in preparation for a funeral.

ON CREMATION

Cremation has been a widespread practice in cultures throughout the world since ancient times, but most of us associate it with Eastern religions. For example, funeral pyres were customary in early India, and the tradition continues today among Hindus and Buddhists. Yet, cremation was common in ancient Greece, the cradle of Western philosophy, for centuries before the birth of Christianity, and it was also practiced in Rome. Though the Israelites generally buried their dead, the bodies of their first royalty, Saul and his sons, were honored by cremation after death in battle. Early Christians adopted the traditional Jewish custom of burial. Over time, the belief that God would resurrect physical bodies became firmly established in both Judaism and Christianity. Religious observers believed that the dead should rest in a tomb until the day when they would be resurrected for an ascent to heaven. As a result, cremation was abhorred by Christians and Jews alike until this century. ■ As early as the middle of the 10th century, distinguished physicians and chemists, primarily from Italy, advocated cremation with no success. The issue was discussed in France, Switzerland, and Britain in the centuries that followed, until the Franco-Prussian War of 1870 - 1871 brought the subject of sanitation and crowding to the notice of the French medical establishment. Again, opposition by religious traditionalists held change at bay. ■ The first Cremation Society, formed to promote the practice of cremation, was founded in England on January 13, 1874. The group, committed to issues of public health and burial reform, supported the development of a crematorium. By the 1890s, cremation was endorsed in Great Britain for those dying of contagious diseases such as diphtheria, cholera, scarlet fever, and tuberculosis. ■ With the firm establishment of Great Britain's Cremation Society, the practice of cremation began to slowly spread throughout the Western world. In the United States, the first cremation was recorded in 1876 in New York. ■ Cremation facilities came to Lakewood Cemetery in 1910, on completion of the Lakewood Cemetery Chapel. Thomas Lowry, a strong supporter of cremation, initiated the project and secured its approval with his fellow trustees. The addition made Lakewood Cemetery the most modern and up-to-date cemetery in the area.

While it was unheard of little more than a century ago, the practice of cremation is rapidly rising in the United States today. Experts predict that cremation rates will double by 2010, while the rate of traditional burials will remain the same.

Lakewood Cemetery, in the heart of Minneapolis, epitomizes the pastoral cemetery that became the ideal in late 19th century North America.

THOMAS B. WALKER (1840-1928)

Pioneer lumberman Thomas Barlow Walker, whose extensive art collection formed the foundation of the Walker Art Center, is buried in Lakewood Cemetery. ■ Walker, born in Xenia, Ohio, in 1840, was a school teacher after completing college, and came to Minneapolis purely by accident when he accepted an offer to trace some lost cargo. He went west to Illinois, Wisconsin, and finally St. Paul, Minnesota, in 1863, where he found the missing merchandise. Once there, he decided to stay in Minnesota, so he took the train on to St. Anthony. ■ Walker's first job was with a government survey office, surveying virgin forests in the north woods. He began to acquire timberlands and set up sawmills throughout the state. Within 10 years, he was among the most wealthy and influential men in Minneapolis. ■ During the 1870s, Walker's interests turned to art. He began collecting to decorate his home, which stood at the corner of Eighth Street and Hennepin Avenue, but his art collection soon outgrew his home. Walker built a gallery between his residence and carriage house and opened it to the public in 1873, the first public gallery in the city. ■ Walker's interests in art broadened in the late 1880s, and he began traveling to London and Paris to acquire paintings by Breton, Bouguereau, and other established European salon painters. In the 1890s, he left his lumber business to his sons and concentrated on attending public auctions and private sales in New York, where he met other major collectors such as J. Pierpont Morgan and Henry Clay Frick. By the early 1900s, Walker possessed one of the world's largest collections of late Chinese jade carvings. At the turn of the century his gallery, now expanded to include the block between Eighth and Ninth Streets, consisted of 14 rooms housing 400 paintings and thousands of art objects. ■ In 1916, Walker and his wife moved to the Thomas Lowry mansion and planned a new gallery to house his vast collection. He began construction of the Walker Art Gallery in November 1924. It opened on May 22, 1927, shortly before his death. The present-day Walker Art Center stands on the same site, which also includes the Guthrie Theater.

At the turn of the century, lumber baron Thomas B. Walker was one of the nation's premier art collectors. His family monument is also a beautiful work of art and is nestled among towering trees.

"Death, the only immortal who treats us all alike, whose pity and whose peace and whose refuge are for all — the soiled and the pure, the rich and the poor, the loved and the unloved."

Mark Twain

MINNEAPOLIS AND THE FOUNDING OF LAKEWOOD CEMETERY

The year 1871, when Lakewood Cemetery was founded, was an eventful one. P. T. Barnum's circus, "The Greatest Show on Earth," opened in Brooklyn, New York; John D. Rockefeller's new Standard Oil Company completed its first year of business; and Mrs. O'Leary's cow started the Great Chicago Fire that nearly destroyed the town. In 1871, Minneapolis had been incorporated as a city for four years and was fast becoming a source of civic pride to the small group of New England settlers guiding its growth.

IN MEMORY OF AN AFFECTIONATE SON, HIS BEREAVED FATHER ERECTS THIS BROKEN COLUMN.

❧ GEORGE DAVIS REDFIELD – DIED 1871

Landmark buildings were beginning to shape the city. The impressive Nicollet House, erected in 1858, was joined in 1871 by the Pence Opera House on Hennepin Avenue and Second Street, and by the magnificent new Academy of Music, on the corner of Hennepin and Washington Avenues. A four-story building, the Academy housed a 1,400-seat auditorium that featured touring plays, concerts, and lectures. Crowds turned out for the nightly attractions — even a spelling bee was a big drawing card.

In 1857, a year before Minnesota became a state, Minneapolis was a sparsely settled town of rough wooden buildings and rutted dirt roads. The main business district was located on Washington Avenue, shown here from Second Avenue South.

COLONEL JOHN H. STEVENS (1839-1889)

Colonel John H. Stevens was the first settler on the west bank of the Mississippi River, where Minneapolis now stands. He came to the Minnesota frontier in 1847, some say 1849. Upon arriving in Minnesota, Stevens was granted the right to settle on the west side in exchange for operating a free ferry across the river for soldiers and army equipment. Stevens, like most early Minnesota settlers, had roots in New England. He was born in 1820, descended from ancestors who fought in the Revolutionary War. An adventurer, Stevens came west in his early 20s, fought in the Mexican War, where he acquired his military rank, then came to St. Anthony before moving across the river. The first permanent dwelling in Minneapolis, Stevens's house became the center of community life — visited by immigrants, hunters, trappers, explorers, and native Americans who lived in the region. The first legal case in the town of Minneapolis was tried at his home. ■ It soon became evident that his farm was destined to become a town. He surveyed and platted the land, laid out city blocks, and gave away many lots to people who were willing to occupy them. ■ Stevens's active role in the development of Minneapolis led to service in numerous public offices, including the Minnesota State Legislature. A brigadier general of the militia, he also commanded troops and volunteers during the Sioux Indian War of 1862. ■ As the city grew and changed, Stevens's house moved from place to place. It now stands at Minnehaha Falls. ■ Stevens's daughter, Mary, was the first Caucasian child born in Minneapolis, in 1849.

In 1854, Colonel John H. Stevens shared the west bank of the Mississippi with native American neighbors. His house (right rear), the first permanent residence in Minneapolis, was eventually moved to a site near Minnehaha Falls, where it now stands.

MINNEAPOLIS BEFORE 1871

The bustling town was a far cry from the primitive military outpost established in the north woods only a few decades earlier. Until the Minnesota Territory opened for settlement in the early 1850s, the area was surrounded by wilderness, inhabited primarily by the Dakota Indians and the adventurers and fur traders who made their way up the Mississippi River or through the Great Lakes.

The first building in Minneapolis was a sawmill erected at St. Anthony Falls in the summer of 1821 to help build Fort Snelling. For the next 27 years, the area remained wild and unsettled. By 1848, the village of St. Anthony contained no more than 300 residents, who all came from the three-year-old lumbering town of Stillwater to operate a sawmill in the heart of the village. These hardy settlers, most of them from Maine, brought their New England traditions with them. They built a church, a school, and a circulating library. Though their houses were reminiscent of New England houses, their daily life was not. According to one historian, their neighbors, the Dakota, who outnumbered the villagers, were "curious and had a habit of wandering in and out of [people's] houses whenever it pleased them."

In 1865, thriving flour and lumber mills operated all along the Mississippi River near St. Anthony Falls.

When it was built in 1858, the Nicollet House, on the corner of Washington and Nicollet, was the most impressive structure in town. By 1890, Minneapolis had grown up around it.

By the early 1850s, St. Anthony had developed into a summer resort, attracting tourists from the East, South, and Europe. An English tourist in 1854 wrote: "The extreme beauty of the scenery...the attractions of the falls...and the comfortable and civilized aspect of the town...render it a fashionable summer resort and picturesque villas are springing up on all available sites." Many visitors decided to stay; by the mid-1850s, settlers from all walks of life were flocking to Minnesota looking for opportunities.

Minneapolis, across the river from St. Anthony, organized its first town council in 1858, the same year Minnesota became a state. Having claimed only 200 residents in 1855, the new town now boasted more than 2,000 people and 446 buildings. Flour milling and lumber industries sprang up, followed by railroads that eventually linked the fledgling town with destinations in all directions.

Charles M. Loring, one of the city's early leaders, was impressed with Minneapolis when he first arrived as a tourist in 1860. On his way to the Nicollet House, Loring said that he crossed the Suspension Bridge, climbed a steep hill, and passed two blocks of one-story wooden stores, fronted by a mud hole called Goose Pond. He was so pleased with the town and the hotel that he decided to stay for the winter. The Nicollet House charged him $6 a week for the room, meals, laundry, and heat for himself, his wife, and son. He admitted that travel was hard because the streets were not cleared, but he liked the town's handsome brick houses and fine stables. He particularly liked the people, whom he found unusually enterprising, cultured, and hospitable. Loring decided to settle down.

By 1870, Minneapolis was booming, with 13,073 residents and plentiful jobs in railroad construction, milling, and manufacturing. Guiding the city's development was a group of civic-minded men, born in the East, who shaped the numerous enduring institutions that mark Minneapolis today. One of those is Lakewood Cemetery.

THE FOUNDING OF LAKEWOOD

In July 1871, Colonel William S. King, businessman and newspaper publisher, had an idea. He approached George A. Brackett, Dorilus Morrison, Charles M. Loring, and other public-spirited community leaders, and proposed that they work together to establish a cemetery where, King said, "the encroachments of the city would never seriously interfere." After an informal meeting, a six-member search committee consisting of Lowry, Dr. C. G. Goodrich, W. D. Washburn, R. B. Langdon, H. G. Harrison, and Dr. Levi Butler was organized to find an appropriate site.

The committee originally chose a tract of land south of the city, where Hennepin Avenue United Methodist Church now stands. But a speculator got wind of the plan and purchased the land, forcing the committee to resume its search. They settled on 130 acres of "gently undulating land" further south between Lake Calhoun and Lake Harriet. Not coincidentally, Colonel King owned the parcel and he agreed to sell it for $21,000, payable over one year at seven percent interest.

On August 7, 1871, Dorilus Morrison called a meeting to organize a cemetery association. Joining Morrison were 14 men, including Colonel King, A. B. Barton, George A. Brackett, W. P. Westfall, R. J. Mendenhall, and the members of the search committee. At this meeting, recorded by Thomas Lowry, the "Lyndale Cemetery Association" was formed. The Association elected officers and a nine-member board of trustees and appointed committees to draft bylaws and to manage financing. Dr. Goodrich was elected chairman of the board of trustees, Mendenhall became treasurer, and Barton was named secretary and superintendent of the cemetery at a salary of $1,500 per year.

By the early 1890s, Lakewood had completed its first stone chapel near the entrance at 36th Street and Hennepin Avenue. The photograph was taken from the top of a hill in Lakewood Cemetery, which at that time was the highest point in Hennepin County.

At a time when $500 could buy a home, the new trustees voted to raise $25,000: $21,000 to cover the purchase price, $4,000 to improve the land. They raised the capital by selling 250 shares of stock at $100 per share and committing to two-thirds of the issue themselves. A committee formed to solicit subscriptions soon sold the balance to other Minneapolitans.

Minneapolis was fertile ground for the ideals and ambitions of the Association's founders, who with their families had emigrated from the East Coast. Some came with great material wealth and influence and some came with little more than a spirit of adventure and sense of purpose. All made their marks on institutions and businesses that continue to thrive today. Many Minneapolis streets, parks, and monuments bear their names.

SO LET ME PASS AWAY, GENTLY AND LOVINGLY, ONLY REMEMBERED BY WHAT I HAVE DONE.

❧ LUCIA ANNE GREENE – DIED 1873

A NEW NAME FOR A NEW INSTITUTION

In his position as superintendent of Lyndale Cemetery, A. B. Barton immediately began corresponding with landscape architects around the country. By April 1872, Barton and the board of trustees had reviewed the candidates and enlisted the services of C. W. Folsom, superintendent of Cambridge's Mount Auburn Cemetery, to develop plans for the grounds.

At the same time, the trustees renamed the new cemetery "Lakewood." The rolling wooded hills and the view of Lake Calhoun undoubtedly provided inspiration for the new name. Perhaps the trustees wanted to emulate the famous cemeteries of the East, like Spring Grove and Green-Wood. Whatever their intention, the name was changed without fanfare and the official reason was never recorded.

By August 1872, surveyors had plotted a portion of the cemetery. The public dedication was held a month later, on September 16, a typical early fall day in Minnesota, with blustery gray clouds scattering showers early in the day. Around noon, families throughout Minneapolis donned their Sunday best and assembled for the trip to Lakewood. Dozens of horse-drawn carriages were seen turning south for the drive on unpaved roads to the lakes. Women in full rustling skirts, gloves, and parasols were escorted by husbands in suits and silk top hats. Children, freshly scrubbed, were on their best behavior.

GREATER LOVE HATH NO MAN
THAN THIS – THAT HE LAY DOWN
HIS LIFE FOR HIS FRIENDS.

    🕊 POOR LITTLE DAVE – DIED 1889

*Nineteen-year-old Maggie Menzel, who died on
January 21, 1872, was the first person buried at
Lakewood Cemetery.*

The spectators and speakers, among them many prominent Minneapolis clergy and civic leaders, gathered on a knoll overlooking Lake Calhoun. At 2 p.m. the ceremony began, led by the Reverend J. H. Tuttle, minister of the Universalist Church. After his welcome and address, Rev. E. S. Thomas, Rector of St. Mark's Church, offered a prayer; Rev. Edward C. Mitchell, pastor of the New Church (Swedenborgan), read a poem written for the occasion, and Rev. Henry N. Payne of the First Presbyterian Church read a selection of scripture. The ceremony also featured a musical quartet and a speech by Dr. Goodrich, representing the new Lakewood Cemetery Association.

In his public address, Rev. Tuttle clearly expressed the community's pride in Lakewood's elegance: "No ancient necropolis of Babylonia, Egypt, or Rome excelled the Père-Lachaise of Paris, Mount Auburn of Boston, or Green-Wood of New York; none of the ancient monuments, shady groves, and winding walks seen in those bygone ages were more skillfully and tastefully wrought than those which meet our eye to-day."

Tuttle also expressed Lakewood's philosophical significance as it was conceived by its founders: "A large, handsome, convenient public cemetery near every large city is a necessity," he asserted. "The refinement, wealth, and social

condition of any city are indicated by the attention that city bestows upon its cemetery."

Public sale of lots began immediately after the dedication. For sale were three grades of lots, measuring 15 by 20 feet, at $50, $100, or $200, depending on location. Sales were brisk. Before the year was out, Lakewood had received its first burial — 19-year-old Maggie Menzel.

The sale of lots totalled $15,135 in 1872, placing the organization on a stable financial footing that allowed rapid repayment of the original investment. Many lots were purchased by families inspired by Lakewood's beauty to disinter their loved ones from other graveyards for reburial on the new grounds.

The management of Lakewood kept pace with the cemetery's rapid growth. In August 1874, the governing association set up its bylaws for the smooth operation of business affairs. Among other things, they made all lot owners voting members of the Association and established costs for services: Opening a grave cost $5, $4 for children under 12; lot repair cost $7 a year; $100 guaranteed perpetual care for the family lot.

COMMUNITY PRIDE MAKES LAKEWOOD STRONG

In August 1875, the Association submitted its first annual report to the lot owners of Lakewood Cemetery. In this report, the trustees noted that sales to date totalled $28,710 with proceeds going to retirement of the original debt, to operating expenses, and to land improvement. Only $9,000 in debt remained. The report quoted landscape architects Adolph Strauch and R. M. Copeland discussing the newly adopted site plan, which according to Superintendent Barton would make Lakewood "the pride of the city." The report stressed the cemetery's nonprofit status. As such, Lakewood would be a public, non-denominational cemetery, available and affordable to the citizens of Minneapolis.

Through Lakewood Cemetery, the founders achieved a common goal — to offer every family and individual an opportunity for proper burial in a beautiful, peaceful environment. They believed strongly in Rev. Tuttle's words spoken that September afternoon in 1872: "Our affection for our friends when living is understood most by the care we take of their graves when they have passed away."

Who were these civic leaders?

Since its founding, Lakewood Cemetery has been carefully tended by skilled groundskeepers, who take pride in creating and maintaining its beautiful landscape.

LABOR WIDE AS THE EARTH HATH ITS SUMMIT IN HEAVEN.

❧ GREAT MILL EXPLOSION MONUMENT – ERECTED 1885

The names of the 18 men killed in Minneapolis's 1878 mill explosion are inscribed on a towering obelisk dedicated to their memory in 1885.

FLOUR MILL EXPLOSION MONUMENT

An Egyptian obelisk erected in 1885 commemorates the death of 18 men killed in the infamous Washburn "A" Mill explosion of May 2, 1878. Built by Cadwallader C. Washburn, the Washburn "A" Mill was the largest flour mill at St. Anthony Falls when it was completed in 1874. Built of limestone, it measured about 90 feet high and 100 feet by 138 feet at the ground. The explosion and fire, which engulfed six mills, was one of the worst disasters in Minneapolis's history. ■ The potential for such disasters is well known. Like grain elevators and cotton gins of that era, flour mills choked the air with a fine, highly combustible dust. Mill workers took the available precautions to avoid accidents — using wooden shovels to avoid creating sparks set off by metal scraping on stone. ■ Nevertheless, on that early spring day, a spark was set off at the enormous "A" Mill on South First Street. The explosion rocked the city like an earthquake. The force of the blast shattered the stone walls and machinery in the mill. Most of the windows on Washington Avenue were broken as were many on Nicollet Avenue. Some reported feeling the shock of the blast in Stillwater. Debris was carried as far as St. Paul. It was later reported that "not one stone was left upon another; and every person engaged in the mill instantly lost his life." Today, a simple tablet marks the location of the catastrophe. ■ On the Mill Workers' monument is etched a sheaf of wheat, a cog, a roller, and a bevel gear with a broken tooth. It bears the words "In memory of those who lost their lives in the Great Mill Explosion May 2, 1878." The names of the 18 mill workers are also etched in the monument's granite face. The men who lost their lives were: E. H. Grundman, George A. Burbank, Charles Henning, Fred A. Merrill, August Schmidt, Henry Hicks, Patrick Judd, William Leslie, Edwin C. Merrill, Ole P. Schie, Clark Wilbur, John E. Rosenius, Peter Hogberg, Jacob V. Rhodes, Charles Kimball, Walter Savage, John Boyer, and Cyrus E. Ewing.

OLD THAUMATURGUS STIRS THE POT

Typical of the group was Colonel William S. King, a native of Malone, New York, who made his name in national politics and earned his rank in the New York State Militia. King moved to Minneapolis in 1859 at age 31 and acquired the *Minnesota Republican*, a St. Anthony newspaper, supposedly the first Republican Party publication in the United States. King soon moved the newspaper across the river to Minneapolis, where it became the city's first newspaper, the *State Atlas*, and achieved fame for King's strong abolitionist views. King championed Liza Winston, a female slave from Mississippi, who sought asylum from her owners while they vacationed at a Lake Calhoun resort. With King's help, Winston escaped to Canada. A barrage of death threats forced the outspoken publisher to spend a night barricaded in his *Atlas* office. Eight years later, King merged the *Atlas* with the *Minneapolis Daily Tribune,* and continued to use the newspaper as a forum for his angry denunciations of slavery and the Democratic Party, which lost favor in Minnesota largely due to King's editorials.

Colonel William S. King.

King was a lifelong champion of Minneapolis who worked tirelessly to improve the city. He built the Calhoun Pavilion in 1877 and later converted it into the Lyndale Hotel, a 75-room, first-class resort hotel, which unfortunately burned down after only two years of operation. In addition, the farsighted King amassed 1,400 acres of land south of Minneapolis during the 1860s. In a time when land was abundant and available for a pittance, residents were shocked to hear that King paid $50 an acre for an 80-acre tract south of the city limits, now in the vicinity of 24th Street. He paid an even more amazing $100 an acre for land near Lake Calhoun and Lake Harriet. King helped finance the Northern Pacific Railroad and inaugurate the city's streetcar system, called the Minneapolis Street Railway Company. An avid supporter of Minneapolis parks, King lobbied unsuccessfully to turn Nicollet Island into a city park, and he later sold and donated land in south Minneapolis to the Minneapolis park system. For his efforts, a grateful Minneapolis public dubbed King "Old Thaumaturgus," an Indian word for miracle worker.

GOOD DOCTOR GOODRICH STARTS FRESH AT 48

One of William King's allies was Dr. Calvin G. Goodrich, a prominent physician and a vehement abolitionist who helped many slaves escape to the North.

In 1880, Col. William S. King's Lyndale Hotel was a popular summer resort. Fire destroyed the hotel, located on the north shore of Lake Calhoun, only two years after it opened.

The son of an eminent attorney from Virginia, Goodrich grew up on his family's Indiana farm. He worked as a surveyor before studying medicine in Cincinnati. At age 48, Goodrich left his home in Oxford, Ohio, where he had built a successful practice as a surgeon and physician, and moved to Minneapolis. He arrived in 1868, with his wife Mary Ann, their children, and a number of freed slaves.

In Minneapolis, Calvin Goodrich built a new medical practice and served as the first president of the Hennepin County Medical Society. He helped organize the Northwestern National Bank (now Norwest Bank), and he invested wisely in various real estate ventures, probably with the help of ambitious Thomas Lowry, who had married Goodrich's daughter, Beatrice, in 1870.

LOWRY TIES THE TOWN TOGETHER

Attorney Thomas Lowry arrived in Minneapolis in 1867 after passing his bar examinations in Illinois. The low demand for legal services made the full-time practice of law unprofitable, so Lowry quickly branched out into other fields. One of his major endeavors was in real estate; his first venture was the

Mr. and Mrs. Thomas Lowry's stately home at Number Two Groveland Terrace was built on a seven-acre rural site at the top of Hennepin Hill, now known as Lowry Hill. It was later purchased by T. B. Walker, who built the Walker Art Center down the hill from the mansion.

development of Lake Street in the mid-1870s. Lowry also anticipated the need for adequate public transportation. He acquired control of the Minneapolis Street Railway Company, which began with a few horse-drawn carts, and in 1886, consolidated the transit systems of Minneapolis and St. Paul into the Twin City Rapid Transit Company. In addition, Lowry participated in the creation of the Minneapolis/St. Paul and Sault Ste. Marie Railroad Company, and was a member of the Minneapolis Library Board. In private life, Mr. and Mrs. Lowry were the toasts of Minneapolis society. Rumors abounded that they spent $100,000 on their house, located at the top of Hennepin Hill, which now borders Minneapolis's Kenwood neighborhood.

BRACKETT BRAVES THE FRONTIER

Unlike Thomas Lowry, George A. Brackett had only a few weeks of formal education, but he did have a similarly adventuresome spirit when he moved from Orono, Maine, to Minnesota in the 1850s. He started out as a butcher, then supplied food to General Sibley's troops during the Sioux Indian War of 1862. Quick thinking and an instinct for survival saved Brackett's life one day when he and a companion were ambushed while buffalo hunting. His friend was killed; Brackett feigned death as the Indians argued over his horse. Left for dead, he hiked back to Fort Atkinson, Nebraska, covering 225 miles of rugged terrain in five days.

After the Civil War, Brackett worked briefly in flour milling, then helped organize the Northern Pacific Railroad with Washburn, King, and Morrison in 1869. Brackett established the Minneapolis Fire Department and became its first volunteer chief. He was an original member of the Minneapolis Park Board and also helped establish the Minneapolis Free Dispensary, which later became the University of Minnesota Medical School. Minneapolis elected George Brackett mayor in 1873.

A rugged individualist, Brackett built his estate on a Lake Minnetonka peninsula and named the adjoining township Orono after his hometown in Maine. That scenic peninsula now bears his name — Bracketts' Point.

Still hardy at age 60, Brackett ventured to Alaska in 1893 to build a wagon road, a four-year endeavor that he personally financed.

AUNT MILLIE BRONSON

In Brackett's family plot at Lakewood lies a friend, Millie Bronson, known for many years as " Aunt Millie" by the Brackett family.

Born into slavery, Aunt Millie was a servant of Confederate General Beauregard during the Civil War. She was captured at the Battle of Tishomingo by Major Brackett of St. Paul, and brought north to Minneapolis. Thereafter, she resided with the Brackett family and cared for the Bracketts' children. She was especially devoted to Annie Brackett, who died in childhood in June 1864.

When Aunt Millie was very old, George Brackett asked if she would like to be buried beside Annie and she gratefully accepted. Millie Bronson was more than 100 years old at the time of her death in March 1885.

HE WELCOMED DEATH, HE LONGED TO BE IN HEAVEN. OH DEATH, WHERE IS THY STING? OH GRAVE, WHERE IS THY VICTORY?

❧ HOWARD KIRK WAKEFIELD — DIED 1882, 14 YEARS OLD

WASHBURN BUILDS A NEW WORLD EMPIRE

George Brackett's boyhood friend, William D. Washburn, grew up in a prominent political family that produced two governors, four members of Congress, a secretary of state, and a foreign ambassador. Washburn attended Bowdoin College in Maine, then studied law before moving west to St. Anthony in 1857. Like Lowry, Washburn found that the practice of law in Minneapolis was not profitable, so he became an agent of the Minneapolis Milling Company, a partnership formed to develop water power on the Mississippi's west bank. The company soon formed the heart of milling and lumber development in the Minneapolis area. Water power made the city, and Washburn's fortune and influence grew.

In 1861, President Abraham Lincoln recognized Washburn's insight and judgment and appointed him Surveyor General of Minnesota. By the early

One of Lakewood's founders, George Brackett organized the Minneapolis Fire Department and served as its first volunteer chief in the 1860s. About 40 years later, firefighters still relied on teams of horses to get to fires quickly. In 1907, the Minneapolis Fire Department raced down Cedar Avenue in answer to a call.

1870s, Washburn's mills were producing 2,500 barrels of flour a day and his lumber business handled 25 million feet of lumber a year.

To move his products, Washburn turned his attention to transportation. He built the first section of the Northern Pacific Railway through Minnesota and helped build the Minneapolis & St. Louis Railroad, the Minneapolis/St. Paul and Sault Ste. Marie Railroad (the Soo Line), and the Minneapolis Street Railway Company. He served as president of the Washburn Orphan Asylum, which was funded by his brother, C. C. Washburn, founder of Washburn-Crosby Company (now General Mills), producer of Gold Medal Flour.

Like others in his family, William Washburn was active in politics. He served in the Minnesota State Legislature in 1858 and 1871, in Congress from 1878 to 1882, and in the United States Senate from 1889 to 1895. In 1883, Washburn built Fair Oaks, a 10-acre estate on 24th Street and Third Avenue South, now the site of Fair Oaks Park across from the Minneapolis Institute of Arts.

YANKEE BECOMES FIRST MINNEAPOLIS MAYOR

Washburn's neighbor and business partner, Dorilus Morrison, was a lively, colorful character in a silk hat who lived at Villa Rosa, a 10-acre estate with elaborate grounds adjacent to Fair Oaks.

Morrison was a merchant and then a successful Maine lumberman before the great pine forests of Minnesota drew him to St. Anthony Falls in 1855. There he joined like-minded men in building the Minneapolis Milling Company, thus beginning a career in business, government, and civic affairs. An enthusiastic supporter of Minneapolis, Morrison became the first president of the Union Board of Trade and actively promoted railroad building through the Union Commercial Association. He served in the Minnesota State Senate in 1864 and 1865, and when Minneapolis became a city in 1867, he was elected its first mayor. (After a year's reprieve, Morrison was re-elected for the one-year post in 1869.)

Pride in his Yankee heritage sparked Morrison's involvement in Minneapolis's New England Society, a social and cultural clan that celebrated its origins with banquets, speeches, and good fellowship. He also worked on the Board of Education, the Park Board, and the Minneapolis Athenaeum, now affiliated with the Minneapolis Public Library.

William D. Washburn.

Dorilus Morrison was an eternal optimist with a carefree attitude. After he became president of Northwestern National Bank in the early 1870s, he had a habit of disregarding his personal bank balance. Much to the chagrin of bank employees, his account was frequently overdrawn, especially in the spring after he paid his lumber crews. When a cashier whispered to him that it was wrong for the president to be overdrawn, Morrison told him to throw out the checks. The cashier protested, "That will look equally bad!" "Well, I guess you'll have to pay them then," Morrison cheerfully replied.

Dorilus Morrison was Minneapolis's first mayor and later president of Northwestern National Bank. In 1875, the bank was a prominent landmark on the corner of First Avenue South and Washington Avenue.

FINDING HEALTH AND WEALTH IN THE NORTHWEST

A summer trip to Minnesota to enjoy the healthful benefits of the clean, crisp outdoors led Dr. Levi Butler to a new life in a city bursting with opportunity.

Butler grew up in Indiana, was educated as a doctor, and practiced medicine for 12 years until his health failed. He first came to Minnesota to recuperate in the summer of 1855. During the next three summers, he bought up pine lands and, at age 41, moved to Minneapolis to enter the lumber business. When the Civil War broke out, Butler raised an entire company for the Third Regiment from the county precincts. He also returned to medicine, serving first as army surgeon and then as surgeon-general before a bout with typhoid fever forced him to resign. Returning to Minneapolis, Butler became a leading force in the lumber trade. By 1875, he was one of the owners of the region's largest pine stands. His sawmill was the biggest in town. His business a success, Butler turned to politics. He was elected to the state senate in 1870, and thereafter became a major promoter of railroad development.

WHEN GABRIEL BLOWS HIS TRUMPET AND THE DAY OF JUDGMENT DAWNS, MY NAME WILL STILL BE WRITTEN ON THIS PIECE OF BRONZE. ❧ WALTER F. HODGE – 1891-1936

RAILROAD TIES MAKE A LADDER FOR LANGDON'S CLIMB

During his career, Robert B. Langdon laid down nearly 7,000 miles of track in nine states and the Northwest Territory. A native of New Haven, Vermont, Langdon started out in 1848 as a railroad construction foreman. He created his own construction business in Wisconsin, then moved to Minnesota in 1858 to break ground for the first Minnesota railroad. Reaching Minneapolis in 1866, Langdon decided to stop moving. He built a canal for the Minneapolis Milling Company and constructed several downtown buildings. Langdon was involved in the management of the Minneapolis & St. Louis and the Minneapolis/Sault Ste. Marie & Atlantic railroads. He was a director of City Bank and a partner in the city's first wholesale grocery business. He served in the Minnesota State Legislature from 1872 to1885 and represented Minnesota three times at the Republican National Convention.

HARRISON BROTHERS TAKE THE TOWN BY STORM

Quick to capitalize on Minneapolis's opportunities were the Harrison brothers — Hugh, Thomas, and William — whose progressive milling family owned the first steam engine in Illinois. Ambitious and well-educated, the brothers arrived in town in 1860. Hugh Harrison, then 38, bought a large, muddy tract (called "the hazel brush thicket" by family members) on the corner of Nicollet and 11th Street. There he built a large family estate; his brothers built nearby. In 1862, Hugh and his brothers built "the Harrison Block" on the corner of Nicollet and Washington in the heart of the business district. Harrison became the second mayor of Minneapolis in 1868. He served on the Minneapolis School Board, gave financial support to Hamline University in St. Paul, and developed many business interests. Like Robert Langdon, Harrison was one of the first organizers of the wholesale grocery business. He helped form B. S. Bull and Company in 1870, then Newell & Harrison Company, predecessor of Super Valu Stores, Inc. In 1878, Harrison and his brothers organized the Security Bank, which soon became the largest banking establishment in the city.

In 1873, "the Harrison Block," at Nicollet and Washington, was 11 years old and still the heart of the Minneapolis business district.

WESTFALL WINS FRIENDS AND INFLUENCES PEOPLE

Banking was the chosen profession of Wilson P. Westfall, who began as a cashier and succeeded partly because he was so well liked. A New York native, Westfall worked in banks in Milwaukee and Prescott, Wisconsin, before signing on as cashier at the National Exchange Bank of Minneapolis in 1867. "Westfall was known in almost every town in Minnesota, Wisconsin, and Dakota," said one historian. "The success of the National Exchange Bank, the second largest in town, was due largely to the personality of its cashier." After establishing himself in Minneapolis, Westfall helped organize the Minneapolis and St. Louis Railway Company in 1870. He teamed up with King, Mendenhall, and Washburn to incorporate the Minneapolis Street Railway Company and was a founding trustee of the Farmers and Mechanics Savings Bank.

MINNEAPOLIS'S FIRST FLORIST, A MAN FOR ALL SEASONS

Surveyor, banker, land agent, florist, botanist, and entomologist, Richard J. Mendenhall was a delightfully eccentric man. A North Carolina native,

In 1890, the Mendenhall Greenhouse, owned by R. J. Mendenhall, was a thriving business located on First Avenue and Eighth Street. Mendenhall, pictured above in a top hat, was one of the founders of Lakewood Cemetery.

Mendenhall had his first taste of the West when he accompanied a cousin to Indiana in pursuit of his uncle's escaped slave. That the slave was never found was a relief, not a disappointment, because Mendenhall had adopted his father's abolitionist views.

Mendenhall later moved west as a surveyor and, after a stint in Iowa, came upriver to St. Paul. At 28, with his boyhood friend Cyrus Beede, Mendenhall formed Beede & Mendenhall, a land, loan, and banking business in Minneapolis. He became president of the State Bank of Minnesota in 1862 and continued as president when it merged with the State National Bank of Minneapolis 10 years later.

Mendenhall served as town treasurer in 1862 and later was named secretary and treasurer of the Board of Education. He also worked with King, Washburn, and Westfall to incorporate the Minneapolis Street Railway Company. But despite his business interests, Mendenhall's passion was science. His published writings on insects were detailed and thorough; in his day, he was considered an authority on that little-known subject. His deep interest in agriculture and horticulture led Mendenhall to build an enormous greenhouse, where he conducted botanical experiments and cultivated a multitude of flowers and other plants. The greenhouse became a business sideline in later years and earned Mendenhall recognition as Minneapolis's first florist.

LORING PLANTS THE SEED FOR MINNEAPOLIS PARKS

Charles M. Loring's passion for horticulture led him in another direction. Loring's love of nature was reinforced by the wild and abundant forests of Maine, where he grew up. His efforts to bring the beauty of nature to all citizens of Minneapolis ultimately distinguished him as "The Father of the Parks."

Loring moved to Minneapolis in 1860 and took a job managing Dorilus Morrison's supply store. He formed his own general store in 1861 with partner Loren Fletcher. In 1866, Loring and other business leaders helped plant trees along Minnehaha Avenue. That same year, Captain Edward Murphy donated to the city 3.3 acres of cow pasture, on which Loring and Murphy planted trees and scored paths to create Minneapolis's first park, now called Murphy Square, at Seventh Street and 22nd Avenue South.

Loring's 35-year service to the Minneapolis Park System began in 1883 when he joined the newly formed Board of Park Commissioners. He chaired the planning committee for Minnehaha Park in 1886 and led the acquisition and

Charles M. Loring in the 1880s.

In the summer of 1890, beautiful walkways and a lake fountain attracted many visitors to Central Park near downtown Minneapolis. Later that year, on December 20, Minneapolis's Central Park was renamed Loring Park, in honor of Charles Loring's lifelong dedication to the Minneapolis Park System.

development team that created the city's park and boulevard system. Throughout his tenure, Loring preferred a hands-on approach. He raised trees from seeds on his land on Lake Minnetonka, transported the seedlings to the city, and personally helped plant them in the new parks. For his outstanding dedication, Central Park was renamed Loring Park in 1890. His last project, Victory Memorial Drive, was planted following his appeal to honor the dead of World War I.

JOHN WESLEY PENCE (1829-1893)

J. W. Pence, a prominent Minneapolis financier, built the Pence Opera House on the corner of Hennepin Avenue and Second Street. The elegant theater opened in 1867, and was the first cultural center in Minneapolis. It was razed in 1952. ■ Pence, a native of Ohio, was a 36-year-old bachelor when he moved to St. Paul in 1865. He had already built a small fortune in farming and livestock by supplying meat and produce to the Union Army during the Civil War. When the war ended, Pence traveled to Minnesota and promptly invested in railroads, banking, and mining. His monument, by the sculptor Caribelli, is entitled "Meditation." It was described as the finest piece of statuary in Lakewood Cemetery at the time.

In 1869, two years after its founding, the Pence Opera House was the cultural center of Minneapolis.

"I am particularly fond of the little groves of oak trees. I love to look at them, because they endure the wintry storm and the summer's heat, and — not unlike ourselves — seem to flourish by them."

Chief Sitting Bull

THE LAND OF LAKEWOOD

Just as Lakewood Cemetery is linked closely to the origins of Minneapolis, the land of Lakewood is also significant to the geological history of Minnesota. Before the Ice Age, the land of Lakewood lay north of the river now known as the Mississippi. With the onset of the new age, glaciers advanced and receded over thousands of years, reshaping the land. Ice creeping up from the southwest first blocked the ancient river channel and altered its course. A new river valley running north and south was created in an interglacial period between the ice advances. Later abandoned by the river, that area appears today as a chain of lakes at the heart of Minneapolis, including Cedar Lake, Lake of the Isles, Lake Calhoun, and Lake Harriet.

Before the immigrant farmers cultivated the prairies, the land was dominated by woods, water, grass, wildlife, and the cultures of the Dakota and the Ojibwa, who were at home in Minnesota centuries before they gave the state its name. A band of Dakota lived in a small village on the eastern shore of Lake Calhoun near the Lakewood site. Today, an ancient Dakota trail linking the lakes with the Mississippi River leads to the gates of Lakewood. It is Hennepin Avenue.

The Dakota inhabited the land where Minneapolis stands long before settlers founded the city. In 1875, three members of the Dakota tribe who resided in the area were photographed at Minnehaha Falls.

Missionary brothers Samuel Pond (left) and Gideon Pond in the 1890s, half a century after they first settled near Lake Calhoun.

In 1834, missionary brothers Samuel and Gideon Pond joined the Dakota at Lake Calhoun, built a tamarack dwelling on a hill near the village, immersed themselves in Dakota culture, and learned their language. Red Eagle and Grizzly Bear, as the missionaries were called, lived for many years a stone's throw from Lakewood Cemetery. A plaque in their honor now stands on the shores of Lake Calhoun near 36th Street.

BARTON MAKES A NEW PLAN

When Superintendent Barton and the Lakewood board chose C. W. Folsom, superintendent of Mount Auburn Cemetery in Cambridge, Massachusetts, to design the grounds of the new Lakewood Cemetery in 1872, the Association was only eight months old. In true Yankee fashion, the founders had purchased land, organized financing, and developed a structure of officers and committees to guide the development of the organization. For his part, Superintendent Barton had plunged into the search for a landscape architect who would realize the founders' vision. Folsom was the logical choice, one which reflected respect for his expertise and reverence for the country's preeminent cemetery, then 40 years old.

In 1873, Superintendent Barton toured Mount Auburn, Green-Wood in New York, Laurel Hill and Mt. Vernon in Philadelphia, Spring Grove in Cincinnati, and Graceland in Chicago to inspect their grounds and confer with their superintendents on landscaping methods. His tour was thorough, and what he found surprised him. He saw landscapes filled with iron fences, hedges, and stone curbings, which clearly defined and enclosed the boundaries of each family lot. To Barton, many of these cemeteries contained "furlongs of cold massive granite crushing all the naturalness and simplicity that remained." As he later reported to the board, "The wealthy vied with each other in their display and expense, but between the fences, terraces, and granite, the old idea of a rural or even a natural cemetery [had] disappeared."

In 1873, Lakewood's founders chose Adolph Strauch's lawn plan as a guide for the cemetery's development.

Only Spring Grove in Cincinnati was different. Its lawn plan, developed by landscape architect Adolph Strauch, reflected a natural beauty and simplicity. "So far as my recommendation is concerned, I answer unhesitatingly in favor of the Cincinnati plan," Barton proclaimed to the board following his return in April 1873. "I saw no grounds that could compare with Spring Grove in beauty of design, and when its spacious lawn is contrasted with the iron fences and heavy stone curbing of the older cemeteries, one would not hesitate a moment as to which they would choose for a last resting place for themselves or their friends." Spring Grove also appealed to the Minnesotan's egalitarian and practical sensibilities — the simplicity of the lawn plan helped eliminate distinctions between the rich and the poor, simplified the cost of maintenance, and helped avoid the problems of neglect that plagued some of the garden cemeteries of the East. Without hesitation, the board dismissed Folsom and his Mount Auburn plan and adopted Barton's lawn cemetery choice.

LAKEWOOD LOOKS EAST

Guided by Strauch's lawn plan, the Association immediately began to develop the existing land and acquire additional property. In the summer of 1874, the members negotiated with Colonel King to buy another 24¾ acres on Lakewood's east side. They signed the bill of sale in 1879, and the same year acquired 2½ acres, north of 36th Street, where they began to build a superintendent's house, a stable, and a dwelling for grounds laborers.

The year 1884 was pivotal for Lakewood. After 13 years, Superintendent Barton stepped down and Ralph D. Cleveland, son of prominent Midwest landscape architect Horace Cleveland, took over. During Cleveland's tenure, Lakewood would evolve to its present form.

In September 1884, Lakewood authorized the purchase of a large section of Minneapolis's Saunders Park neighborhood, now incorporated in Lakewood's northeast section. When the Association first began this acquisition, Saunders Park's streets were sprinkled with houses. But the residents were willing to vacate or move their homes to nearby lots, and the Lakewood property line crept east of Hennepin Avenue along 36th Street. Later that year, the Minneapolis Roads and Bridges Council asked the Lakewood Association for permission to extend Hennepin Avenue south of 36th Street, right through the cemetery. The Association denied the request, and Hennepin Avenue came to rest once and for all at the cemetery's gates.

Actually, gates were not there at that time. They were constructed three years later, in 1887, after much debate over the best site for the main entrance. The board originally chose to put the entry gates and administration building on Humboldt Avenue at 36th Street, then came to prefer a second choice — Hennepin and 36th Street — which Dorilus Morrison vehemently opposed. Though the Hennepin entrance was eventually approved, Morrison wanted the record to state: "All present voted 'aye,' with the exception of Mr. Morrison, who wished an emphatic 'no!' recorded for him."

With its sights set on expanding to the east, the Association continued to acquire land in Saunders Park. In 1893, Lakewood purchased another 50 acres, which included 259 lots and 17 dwellings. Owned by Charles M. Loring, Henry F. Brown, and James J. Hill, the land was sold to the Association for $90,000, with $40,000 down and the balance payable over four years. The neighborhood's remaining property was purchased in smaller parcels during the next two decades. One by one, houses were dismantled or simply moved to other locations. By the time the acquisitions ended, Lakewood had grown from its original 130 acres to its present 250 acres.

DEATH LIES ON HER LIKE AN UNTIMELY FROST UPON THE SWEETEST FLOWER OF ALL THE FIELD.
᠀ MINNIE SUTHERLAND – DIED 1875 – 17 YEARS OLD

In 1905, the intersection of Calhoun Boulevard and 36th Street was still a dusty rural road, far from the bustle of the growing city.

Not often seen, deer, fox, and other wildlife leave telltale tracks in Lakewood's winter landscape.

THE BOY AND THE DEER

As a 35-year employee of Lakewood Cemetery, Grounds Superintendent Jim Ostvig has witnessed countless funerals. Yet the memory of one still brings tears to his eyes. ■ In the 1970s, the deer population was wreaking havoc on Lakewood's gardens — eating and trampling the tender young bedding plants. With much effort, the grounds crew finally managed to chase the deer out of the cemetery. ■ One female deer remained, and she became a cemetery mascot. Jim and others tried to lure her close with bits of food, but she was too skittish. She would dart away at the sight of a human being. ■ One morning, the funeral for a 10-year-old boy was scheduled at Lakewood. A hearse carrying the boy's casket pulled up near the open grave and the family began to arrive. As members of the funeral procession parked their cars and assembled, Lakewood's lone deer suddenly appeared out of the trees and walked calmly toward the hearse. As the crowd watched, the deer walked up to the window of the hearse, stopped, and peered in at the small casket lying there. Then it slowly turned and left the group. As Jim recalls, the parents accepted the visit as a gift — a special sign. "Now we know that he's accepted in Heaven," they said of their son.

WE LOVED HER, BUT JESUS LOVED HER MORE. ❧ MILDRED HASSELGRIN – 1903-1918

ENHANCING NATURE'S GIFTS

Lakewood's aggressive expansion was necessary to accommodate the anticipated needs of a growing metropolis. With that in mind, the Association was equally ambitious in its efforts to improve the land it acquired.

One colossal effort took place in 1913 under the direction of Superintendent Arthur W. Hobert. That year, Lakewood began a $100,000 project to convert a 15-acre swamp into a picturesque lake. The project's success depended on the raw muscle of men and horses, and on the power of simple tools. With permission from the Minneapolis Park Board, Lake Calhoun was dredged by the city in August; the resulting 177,000 cubic yards of sand and gravel were used to fill in seven acres of the swamp. The swamp water was drained into neighboring Lake Harriet. The LaCrosse Dredging Company was hired by the Association to dig a new lake. Horse-drawn wagons pulling scraper boxes, and drag-line dredging equipment and laborers wielding picks and shovels dug down 80 feet to create the

The crab apple trees that dot the shores of Lakewood's peaceful lake bring a profusion of pink blossoms every spring.

new lake basin. After two years of hard labor, what had been the "mosquito and malaria breeding hole" condemned in Minneapolis newspapers had been turned into a lovely eight-acre lake, surrounded by graceful new grounds. The beautiful new lake put to shame a nearby small body of water, named the Duck Pond, which was filled in 12 years later.

In gratitude for the city's help in constructing the lake, the Lakewood Cemetery Association donated a 40-foot-wide strip of land between 36th and 38th Streets for an extension of King's Highway, a major thoroughfare to the areas south of the city.

HE WALKED WITH GOD, AND HE WAS NOT, FOR GOD TOOK HIM. ❧ ROBERT P. HERRICK – 1857-1915

THE CASE OF THE TRICKY FISH

In 1926, Lakewood's lake caused a stir among city officials when they discovered that an underground stream connected the lake with Lake Harriet. Particularly disturbed was Park Commissioner Emil Youngdahl, who claimed that the emigrant fish were promoting illegal activity among otherwise respectable citizens.

"I know of persons who sneak away from their wives and children in the early morning and go to that pool and fish," Youngdahl complained. "One person caught a big string the first time he went, but the second time the caretaker caught him."

The problem was keeping the fish in Lake Harriet where they belonged. Commissioner Frank Gross offered a wry solution: "Why not ask the Izaak Walton League to put up a sign in fish language, asking them to move into [Lake Harriet] during the summer and stay there until spring?"

The matter was referred to Park Board Superintendent Theodore Wirth for investigation. Charges against the errant fishermen were never filed.

KING + LAKEWOOD = LYNDALE PARK

Lakewood's long-standing association with the Minneapolis Park Board brought benefits to the board, Lakewood, and city residents. In 1890, a year that saw park development boom with the expansion of Loring Park, acquisition of Powderhorn Park, and construction of Interlachen Parkway (now William Berry Parkway, between Lake Calhoun and Lake Harriet) Lakewood gave the city a 35-acre parcel of woods and wetlands along the cemetery's south side.

Lakewood's gift to Minneapolis provided the foundation for Lyndale Park, today one of the most notable and popular parks in the city. Following Lakewood's lead, Colonel King donated adjacent property in 1891, thus positioning the 61¼-acre park between Lake Harriet, King's Highway, and Lakewood Cemetery.

Lyndale Park's Rose Garden is the second oldest municipal rose garden in the United States, after the garden in Hartford, Connecticut. Creation of the garden began in 1907, under the tutelage of Theodore Wirth, lured by Charles Loring from his position in Hartford to oversee the project. Wirth installed more than 4,000 plants (250 varieties) at a cost of slightly more than $3,000. A half-century later, the park's fountains were put in place: first the bronze and marble Heffelfinger Fountain from the Villa Montalto near Florence, Italy, then the Phelps Fountain, originally located in downtown Minneapolis.

The growing popularity of rock gardens prompted Wirth to build the Lyndale Park Rock Garden. In 1929, he shipped in 350 tons of moss- and lichen-covered rock from Wisconsin's Diamond Bluff on the St. Croix River. In 1936, the area between the rock garden and Lakewood Cemetery was named the Thomas Sadler Roberts Bird Sanctuary. The rock garden fell into disrepair in the late 1940s but was revived and rebuilt beginning in 1983.

Lakewood's flower beds are a combination of beauty and precision. At 36th Street and Lake Calhoun Parkway, passersby get a glimpse of Lakewood spelled out in silver santolina and begonias.

Johann Emil Oberhoffer conducted the Minneapolis Symphony Orchestra in 1910, seven years after he guided its founding.

JOHANN EMIL OBERHOFFER (1867-1933)

Violinist and composer Johann Emil Oberhoffer was born in Munich, Bavaria, the son of a musical family. At an early age, he took music lessons from his father, an organist, and by age 10 he was a proficient violinist. Oberhoffer also studied piano in both Munich and Paris, and toured as orchestra conductor with a traveling company that was presenting the Passion Play. ■ In 1885, Oberhoffer emigrated to America and settled in New York, where he was music director at Manhattan College. He moved to Minneapolis in 1897, and quickly involved himself in musical affairs. His first position was as conductor of the Schubert Club Chorus and Orchestra of St. Paul, and director of the Minneapolis Apollo Club. In 1901, he became director of the Philharmonic Club of Minneapolis and began organizing a permanent symphony orchestra by contributing his own money and soliciting endowments from others. Oberhoffer conducted the first Minneapolis Symphony Orchestra on November 5, 1903. Though it began as a group of 60 musicians, it quickly grew to fully symphonic proportions. ■ Oberhoffer conducted the Minneapolis Orchestra for 19 years. After retiring in 1923, he appeared as guest conductor of the Los Angeles Philharmonic Orchestra and the San Francisco, St. Louis, and Detroit Symphonies, and as conductor of concerts at the Hollywood Bowl. ■ Musical notes are carved into the base of the obelisk that marks Oberhoffer's grave, a monument to Minneapolis's historic conductor.

WATER, WATER EVERYWHERE, BUT...

Lakewood Cemetery is nearly surrounded by lakes, but the beautiful landscape requires running water to irrigate its lawns, trees, and gardens. In 1885, the search began to find the artesian well that many people believed was on the property. Search they did, all over and straight down. The Lakewood Association spent nearly $12,000 digging a well 2,150 feet deep. At the time, it was cited by the U.S. Geological Survey as the deepest well ever dug in Hennepin County. Unfortunately, it was so deep that there were no pumps available to bring the water to the surface. In 1904, the Association constructed a water tower on Lakewood's highest hill, which irrigated the grounds until 1955. When it was torn down, 60 feet of earth was shaved from the top of the hill and used to fill and level sections of the adjacent land. Lakewood Cemetery was no longer the highest elevation in Hennepin County.

At first, Lakewood's proximity to Lake Calhoun provided an abundant source of free water. Pumped from the lake into the tower, the water gravity-fed the grounds and gardens. But in 1913 the practice was called into question by the *Minneapolis Journal*, which reported that Lakewood was using as much as 300,000 gallons of water a day. The link to Calhoun not only gave Lakewood more than $2,000 worth of water, said city officials, but threatened to lower water levels in the city's lakes and, ultimately, in Minnehaha Falls. Thereafter, Lakewood supplied its water needs from its own on-site wells. Today the cemetery operates four wells on its grounds. Only the Administration Building is connected to the Minneapolis water system.

ASLEEP IN JESUS: BLESSED, FROM WHICH NONE EVER WAKE TO SLEEP.

᠉ CHRISTIAN ROMPAC – SEPT. 20, 1826-FEB. 2, 1898

LANDSCAPES MAKE LAKEWOOD ONE OF A KIND

The trees, shrubs, and gardens that form Lakewood's botanical landscape provide a living laboratory for the study of science. Like Mount Auburn Cemetery, which provided botanists and horticulturists with an arboretum, Lakewood gives students and scholars a site for plant study and experimentation.

In 1871, little was known about the survival of non-native trees and plants in the Minnesota climate. Lengthy experimentation was necessary and Lakewood committed itself to the task by securing plants from all over the country. Varieties of maple, oak, ash, and other species made the slow journey north by rail

Lakewood's Section 17 offers a restful atmosphere that encourages quiet reflection.

to Lakewood, where they were planted to test their hardiness. Nursery managers came to the cemetery to learn about the plants' adaptability to climate and disease. Over time, Lakewood contributed to the body of knowledge on various exotic plants. As a bonus, the cemetery now possesses a number of plant species found nowhere else in the state. Before the University of Minnesota established its arboretum near Chanhassen in 1958, university students made field trips to Lakewood every fall to study and identify unusual plant species.

FIELDS OF FLOWERS IN FEBRUARY

In 1886, two young men named Wesling and Hartman started a greenhouse, which they located south of Hennepin and 36th Street in Saunders Park. After only two years in business, however, Wesling pulled up stakes and built his own greenhouse further south. When the Association acquired the Saunders Park neighborhood in 1888, Hartman's greenhouse went with it — and Lakewood Cemetery entered the greenhouse business.

Operation of an on-site cemetery greenhouse was not common in those early days. In 1892, only 20 of the 83 member cemeteries in the Association of American Cemetery Superintendents operated greenhouses — nine of which were in Massachusetts, undoubtedly influenced by Mount Auburn.

Landscape architecture and gardening were central to cemetery management at the turn of the century. By 1895, Lakewood was spending $1,000 a year for bedding plants and flowers, and Superintendent Hobert, who replaced Cleveland in 1891, was convinced that expanding the greenhouses was necessary. Operating a greenhouse of any size was extremely difficult and expensive at the turn of the century, yet at one time Lakewood maintained six enormous greenhouses that together spanned 73,000 to 100,000 square feet of growing space. (Today a typical greenhouse occupies 15,000 square feet.) Each house was 60 feet wide by 320 feet long — longer than a football field. Coal-fed boilers produced steam to heat the huge glass houses through the cold Minnesota winters. Stoking the fires was a 24-hour-a-day job and Lakewood employed one man for each of two shifts. The job was simple but not easy — shoveling coal for 12 hours, seven days a week. Thermostats were unavailable until late in the 1920s, so once an hour someone had to walk the aisles of every greenhouse to read the thermometers and adjust the valves to maintain the proper temperature.

During peak years, many workers were employed in the Lakewood greenhouses, which grew a wide variety of cut flowers for funerals, memorials, and the wholesale and retail trade. Prior to 1924, Lakewood operated a thriving business as the largest wholesale cut-flower supplier in the city, making flower deliveries all over town. Lakewood's success raised the ire of local Minneapolis florists, who complained that tax exemptions gave Lakewood an unfair competitive advantage. A successful lawsuit and trial, and a subsequent injunction, brought Lakewood's wholesale and retail florist services to a halt.

IN HEAVEN WE SHALL KNOW ALL.
ఎ&ు GEORGE M. BRYANT –
NOV. 27, 1834 - JAN. 23, 1893

In 1925, Lakewood's spacious retail greenhouse showroom displayed cut flowers and arrangements for sale to cemetery visitors. Lakewood also operated the largest wholesale flower business in the city until 1924, when a lawsuit by Minneapolis florists ended the practice.

Today, Lakewood's greenhouses produce plants for 50 flower beds, more than 1,500 monument urns, and cut-flower bouquets for visitors. The cemetery runs one of the largest cemetery greenhouse operations in the country.

Shortages of labor and materials during World War II forced the greenhouse to cut operations by nearly half. After the war, Superintendent Paul Anderson scaled down the operation again by selling four of the largest greenhouses, which were dismantled and shipped to their new owners.

More recently, the energy crisis of the 1970s brought abrupt changes to the entire floral industry. Heating bills skyrocketed and labor costs increased. These economic pressures put many cemetery greenhouses in the red and eventually drove most of them out of business. Lakewood's greenhouse also lost money at that time, but management took the long view. New technologies doubled window insulation values. Shutting down the large greenhouse in January and February halved heating costs. At the same time, Lakewood began to purchase seedlings from other suppliers, thus guaranteeing yields and eliminating labor-intensive planting from seeds.

Today, Lakewood still boasts one of the largest cemetery greenhouse operations in the United States, planting more than 95,000 flowers each season. The cemetery is also the leading buyer of bulbs in Minnesota. "We plant nearly 30,000," says Greenhouse Manager Paul Aarestad. Quality remains the primary consideration. "We spend $6,000 every year purchasing, planting, and covering tulips. Then we pull them all up and plant new bulbs in the fall. That guarantees uniformity in size and bloom," Aarestad explains. "It's a long-standing tradition."

Tradition also dictates the design of Lakewood's formal flower beds. Most beds have featured the same flowers in the same locations for decades. Red tulips at the front entrance provide a familiar splash of color every spring. Lakewood's canna lilies adorn the entrance every summer, as they have for 100 years. (Cuttings taken each season allow Lakewood to propagate a variety that is no longer available elsewhere.)

Why does Lakewood perpetually maintain these particular arrangements? "If I change the color of a flower bed, people let me know," says Aarestad. "They have a personal connection with Lakewood. We respect that."

CONTINUING THE TRADITION

Today, careful tending, more growing space, and an extended growing season mean that Lakewood can produce larger plants with a profusion of blooms. These top-quality blooms and greens bring satisfaction to lot owners, visitors, and employees alike.

The greenhouse sells fresh floral bouquets, potted plants, Easter lilies, poinsettias, and evergreen wreaths according to the season. These items, sold to visitors for placement on graves, can also be placed by Lakewood staff on request. If the lot owner sets up a standing order, the greenhouse will fill an urn, trim shrubs, or place a bouquet at the specified time. Lot owners can also opt to invest in the Special Care Fund: Interest from the investment pays for flowers and upkeep of a designated lot.

The greenhouse staff also plants and maintains the numerous cast-iron urns that adorn lots throughout the cemetery. Simple or ornate, small or as large as six feet in diameter, urns were popular from the earliest days to the 1960s, when Lakewood tended more than 3,000. Today, the cemetery works on about 1,500 urns each year.

Brilliant red tulips at Lakewood's 36th Street entrance have been a tradition for decades.

Minnesota's climate puts pressure on the greenhouse crew every spring, when workers try to set up the urns and about 50 formal flower beds by Memorial Day. Every year the spring crew is called back in February; by May, 16 additional people are on the payroll. When the danger of hard frost is past, only a few weeks remain to bring spring color back to Lakewood for Memorial Day, traditionally the cemetery's biggest visiting day.

BUSY AS A GROUNDSKEEPER

In addition to the greenhouse staff, Lakewood employs a separate grounds crew that faces the daunting task of grooming and nurturing Lakewood's 250 acres and maintaining more than 100,000 monuments and markers. Their efforts are visible everywhere — the grounds of Lakewood rival those of any of Minneapolis's finest parks and boulevards. That accomplishment is even more impressive when one realizes that for the first eight decades of Lakewood's history, maintenance was done by hand, without benefit of the machines and power tools we now take for granted.

A formal flower bed at Lakewood is filled with canna lilies, African marigolds, and petunias in preparation for Memorial Day, the biggest visiting day of the year at the cemetery.

SIR JOSEPH FRANCIS (1801-1893)

One of the oldest and most celebrated monuments at Lakewood Cemetery is that of businessman and inventor Sir Joseph Francis. His epitaph reads, "Joseph Francis, Father and Founder of the United States Life Saving Service. Founder of American Ship-wreck Society 1842. Inventor of Corrugated Metallic Life Car, Life Boat, &c. Received the thanks of the 49th Congress, honored by the 50th Congress for his service to humanity. Honored, decorated, rewarded and knighted by the Crowned Heads of Europe. Born March 12, 1801." ■ Although Francis and his wife, Ellen, lived in New York, they vacationed in Minneapolis before Lakewood Cemetery was founded. According to legend, as Ellen Francis stood on the hill one day, looking west over Lake Calhoun, she said to her husband that she had never seen so beautiful a spot, and she wished that it might be her final resting place. When the cemetery was laid out, Francis immediately purchased the lot on the northwest corner where she had stood — Lot 1, Section 1. When Ellen Francis died in 1878, she was buried on the grassy hill she had chosen. ■ At one time, the tomb was shaded by a weeping willow, which grew from a slip Francis brought from Napoleon's tomb at St. Helena in 1877. It grew into a tree at Lakewood. ■ In his 1893 book, *The History of Minneapolis*, Isaac Atwater said, "Mr. Francis is still living but quite advanced, being over 91 years old. He spends most of his time in summer sitting by his wife's tomb, and explaining to visitors points of interest about the cemetery. His own epitaph is already chiseled on a granite slab that inclines downward from his wife's tomb." He died that same year, May 10, 1893.

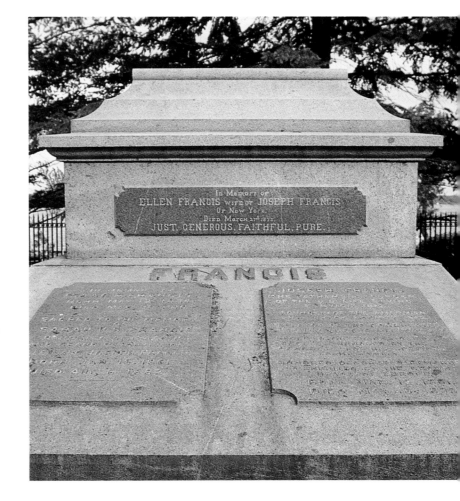

New York inventor Sir Joseph Francis chose Lakewood Cemetery at the request of his wife, Ellen, who vacationed with him in Minneapolis in the 1860s. When the cemetery was founded, Francis bought the first lot, overlooking Lake Calhoun.

White begonias and New Guinea impatiens make a stunning floral display in one of Lakewood's many formal flower gardens.

THE LONG AND WINDING ROAD

"We've got a beautiful lake and groves of trees, but it's the roads that really set us apart from other cemeteries," Lakewood Grounds Superintendent Jim Ostvig recently said. Lakewood's 11 miles of roads are wide and well kept as they wind through the 250-acre grounds. Like so many aspects of Lakewood, these attractive roads were planned decades ago and built by workers aided by horses and wagons.

As far back as 1871, road construction at Lakewood provided winter jobs for the seasonal grounds workers who were laid off in the fall. During World War I, grounds worker Anton Bergstrom, and others like him, hauled rock with horse-drawn wagons to build solid roadbeds in the cemetery. The rock came up the Mississippi River on barges and then was loaded on wagons for the trip to Lakewood. On the coldest, harshest days of the winter, with temperatures dipping to 15 to 20 degrees below zero, workers rode those open wagons. To keep warm, Bergstrom walked behind the horses with reins in hand. But he said, "I always caught a mighty chill on Hennepin Avenue," because cars forced him to drive the team faster, which he could only do from his wagon perch.

MAKING ENDS MEET

During the Depression, when jobs were scarce, Lakewood hired 90 to 100 workers each summer to maintain the grounds. There was no shortage of labor. One summer in the early 1930s, one of the Minneapolis Millers, Minneapolis's professional hockey team, signed on as a grounds worker to earn extra money. Multimillion-dollar contracts and product endorsements did not exist, and he was delighted to have a job. Word spread and before long, the whole hockey team was keeping fit working at Lakewood. They came back, summer after summer.

Though machines were not available to simplify tasks, variety — and a healthy competitive spirit — added a little spice to each day's efforts. Every man was assigned a section which he maintained — mowing, trimming, planting, and watering. Shovels, wheelbarrows, and watering cans were the tools of the trade, along with push mowers to cut the lawn and sheep shears to trim around monuments. Workers vied with each other to maintain the best section.

Veteran groundskeepers are not likely to reminisce fondly over "the good old days." In 1916, Lakewood paid its laborers $2.50 per day for 10 hours of work, and upped the day's pay only 25 cents the next year. By 1920, laborers were

Sunny yellow tulips create a cheerful splash of springtime color near the lake.

earning $4.05 per day for nine hours of work. Wages remained at that rate for 16 years, then jumped a nickel per hour. The modern era, ushered in by World War II, brought changes for workers throughout the nation. Lakewood labor negotiations, which began in 1942, brought increased security and prosperity to its workers.

Supervising nearly 100 men spread across 250 acres was a formidable challenge for the Lakewood superintendent and grounds foreman in the days before easy transportation and instant communication. Don Strickland, greenhouse superintendent from 1965 to 1978, watched six teenagers hired to water the grounds sneak off for an afternoon in Lake Harriet. At 5 p.m. they came to collect their pay.

"Did you do a good job?" asked Strickland.

"Yes, we watered everything," one of the boys answered.

"Well, come on in and get your check," Strickland said. "I punched you out at quarter to one when you went swimming."

MACHINES AND THE MODERN AGE

The post-World War II era marked a turning point in cemetery grounds management. Superintendent Paul Anderson, whose 47-year career began in 1925, brought Lakewood into the age of labor-saving machines — but not without a struggle. "It will never work!" grumbled Grounds Superintendent Roy Nelson when Anderson proposed replacing shovels with a backhoe in the early 1950s. "We can't work in those sections with that big machine."

A Lakewood urn spills over with a generous variety of flowers and vines, including petunias, vincas, coleus, daisies, geraniums, and other plants. Every spring, the greenhouse staff plants about 1,000 urns throughout the cemetery.

But progress won over tradition. Today, opinions have reversed. "The backhoe is the greatest machine ever invented for cemeteries," says today's Grounds Superintendent Jim Ostvig. David Hatlestad, president of Lakewood until 1989, agrees: "Now, of course, if the guys had to dig a grave with a shovel, as their predecessors did... Well, they wouldn't do it!"

The impact of machinery is also evident if you glance at Lakewood's payroll. Gone are the days of the 100-man grounds crew. Lakewood now employs 30 to 40 seasonal workers in the peak season, from early spring to late fall. Tractors, backhoes, and other power equipment enable the cemetery to operate with a 10-person crew through the winter months.

Despite the much-reduced labor force, land management is still an expensive business. To prepare and open a new section of land may require a host of chores — soil sampling, road removal, grading, filling, sprinkler installation, new road building and curbing, seeding, and landscaping. In 1982, the sprinkling system for just one of Lakewood's more than 50 sections cost more than $20,000.

MAY THE LORD WATCH BETWEEN ME AND THEE WHEN WE ARE ABSENT ONE FROM THE OTHER. ❧ VIRGINIA G. SCOTT – 1922-1976

NATURE TAKES A TOLL

The forces of nature can add to the cost. In the early 1950s, an eight-inch rainstorm with high winds flooded the cemetery and uprooted trees. A tornado in 1979 damaged or destroyed 450 trees; two years later, a second tornado destroyed another 250. While some were split or broken, many were ripped out of the ground, tearing up underground sprinkling systems and tipping or damaging monuments. Removing downed trees and stumps and repairing the damage isn't easy. The city granted Lakewood a burning permit after the 1979 tornado; fires burned night and day for three months. To restore the land, the cemetery had to plant hundreds of trees at $300 apiece.

The cemetery has also had to contend with Dutch Elm disease, which arrived in the late 1970s to claim nearly 700 majestic elms. The drought of 1988 spared Lakewood's trees but virtually destroyed the grass. Most of the 250 acres had to be restored with new sod or seed.

A HAVEN IN THE CITY'S HEART

Nature may be occasionally rough on Lakewood, but Lakewood and its employees are good to nature. For example, during 1988 and 1989, greenhouse and grounds workers nurtured 100 newly hatched pheasants. But the easy pickings boosted Lakewood's fox population, which thrives in the lush quiet surroundings.

Today, the cemetery is a haven for fox, rabbits, owls, pheasants, songbirds, and falcons. Season by season, Lakewood provides a stage where the balance of nature is played, oblivious to the fast-paced bustle of the city outside.

LIMITLESS LAND?

Despite its great size, Lakewood is not limitless, nor can it grow as it once did. How much more space is left at Lakewood? The question has been asked for decades and the answer is remarkably the same: "I asked Paul Anderson that question when I came here in 1950," says David Hatlestad. "He said Lakewood has space for 50 to 60 more years. Well, 40 years later, I still say we have 50 to 60 years left." The enduring nature of Lakewood Cemetery will continue well into its second century.

Sparkling snow and ice-glazed branches create a spectacular winter scene at Lakewood Cemetery.

"Custom is lord of all mankind."

Aleksandr Pushkin

Rules, Rituals, and Remembrance

In 1875, after four years of reflection on how to best serve the public need, the Lakewood Cemetery Association published its original bylaws.

This document gave lot owners voting power to select trustees and to set basic rules regarding the cemetery's costs and operations. A $5 fee was required for a burial. The bylaws established provisions for tomb construction, public lot burial, and maintenance funding. A $50 payment guaranteed perpetual care by the cemetery, or lot owners could choose to pay $5 annually. The 215 individuals and families who owned lots could hire outside workmen to make improvements under Lakewood supervision.

The 16 original rules and regulations were of great importance to these proprietors, most of whom assumed personal responsibility for the maintenance of their lots. Keeping everyone satisfied, however, was a difficult task. As one owner candidly said at the time, "I would like to do as I please with my own lot, but I would not like to give my neighbor the same privilege."

One of those privileges regarded tree planting. Most early lot owners planted from one to five trees, a practice which threatened to transform Lakewood into a forest. To prevent this, the first rule laid down by the Association prohibited lot owners from planting trees. Anticipating the indignant outcry, the Association backed up its decree with numerous quotes from distinguished authorities who warned against the "evils" of injudicious tree planting.

MY ONLY REGRETS ARE THE TEMPTATIONS I HAVE SUCCESSFULLY RESISTED.

❧ CLYDE EARL HAGEN – 1901-1974

DON'T TREAD ON ME

Today, a panoramic view reveals a seemingly random placement of monuments and headstones. But examination of a plot map proves otherwise. The first Lakewood sections were laid out like city blocks, with numbered even and odd sides of the street and alleyways. Prevailing mores affected this design. When Lakewood was begun, it was considered a terrible thing to walk on someone's grave, so Lakewood built alleys to prevent that. Today, space considerations and changing customs abrogate the need for the alleys.

A FAMILY AFFAIR

For decades, Lakewood Cemetery drew visitors as if it were a city park. People brought in baskets of lunch and strolled through the grounds, enjoying the scenery and reading the epitaphs. Families came out on weekends to spend the day picnicking on the grounds near the family lot.

The streetcar running along the west side of the cemetery made visiting easy for Twin Cities residents. For a nickel, people could ride all the way from downtown to the cemetery, which had deeded the streetcar company a right-of-way for that purpose. "When I was a kid in the 1920s, we didn't have a car, so the

In its early years, Lakewood Cemetery, like spacious lawn cemeteries in other growing cities, was a favorite spot for people seeking a lovely, park-like atmosphere. Visitors with picnic lunches, books, and blankets viewed a trip to Lakewood as an all-day outing.

whole family packed a lunch and boarded the streetcar bound for Lakewood," recalls Wally Nelson, who later worked there. "We went out to visit the grandparents — it was a big event."

Over the years, Lakewood's rules and bylaws were revised or expanded to meet changing needs and customs. A revision in 1889 reserved Sunday visits for lot owners and their families, who were required to present admission tickets at the gate. Because visitors tended to linger, Lakewood provided camp chairs to make them more comfortable.

HIS SMILE WILL FOREVER LIGHT UP OUR HEARTS.

JOHN ALBERT SCHOEBERL – JULY 10, 1984 - OCT. 11, 1988

THE FAMILIAR FACE OF DEATH

Such close and frequent association with a cemetery may strike people today as strange. But the custom of cemetery visitation underscored a very different understanding of life and death in those times. For the first half-century of Lakewood's existence, death was an everyday presence. Average life expectancies were short. Unlike today, when the average life expectancy is around 74 years, the average life expectancy in 1900 was only 47 years. Unchecked disease, especially in the young, kept those averages down.

In 1895, the popular Lake Harriet Streetcar linked Lakewood Cemetery with the rest of Minneapolis. Visitors boarding downtown could ride all the way to the cemetery's Lake Calhoun stop for only a nickel.

More than half of all deaths occurred in people under 40. In 1908, 16 percent of Minneapolis children died before their first birthday. Another 16 percent died before age 19, and 20 percent more died before age 40. Only 25 percent of the population reached 60 years of age. Tuberculosis and pneumonia were the leading causes of death; smallpox and diphtheria were also dangerous threats. The flu epidemic of 1919 struck without warning and killed millions worldwide.

Death a century ago was definitely an everyday family affair. Only five percent of all Americans passed away in a hospital, where today more than 70 percent spend their final days. When illness struck, people were cared for at home with the help of a visiting doctor. And at home they died, surrounded by family and friends. Survivors young and old personally experienced life's passing.

Familiarity with dying and death drew people to Lakewood Cemetery. It served for a great many as an institution of personal significance, at which rituals and traditions in burial, mourning, and commemoration helped comfort the grieving and heal the rift left by a painful loss.

In 1905, funeral directors dressed in formal mourning attire led most funeral processions in horse-drawn hearses. Processions often began at the home of the deceased, where funeral services were conducted in the family parlor.

FLOWERS FOR REMEMBRANCE

After tree planting was prohibited, families beautified the graves of friends and loved ones with flowers, shrubs, and urns. Each spring they came to Lakewood laden with seeds, plants, tools, and watering cans to cultivate the graves. At Christmas time, family members thatched graves with evergreen boughs. Despite the good intentions, some lots ran wild, others went barren. Maintenance became a problem. Lot owners were periodically reminded to remove watering cans and other tools from the grounds.

So, in 1916, after 45 years of debate and discussion, the Association ended the practice of independent plantings. On Decoration Day that year, the Lakewood staff met hundreds of visitors bearing shrubs and potted plants at the entrance gates and informed them that planting and cultivating of lots was no longer permitted. Instead, visitors were invited to leave cut flowers in built-in vases at the grave site. For those who chose to pay an additional fee to the Permanent and Special Care Funds, flowers, urns, and wreaths would be placed on graves by the cemetery staff.

After it was founded in 1868, Decoration Day (which later became Memorial Day) was a patriotic holiday honoring America's soldiers. On Decoration Day in 1924, Minnesota regiments in full uniform paraded through the streets of Minneapolis.

MEMORIAL DAY

Originally called Decoration Day, our traditional Memorial Day holiday was established in 1868 by General John A. Logan, then Commander-in-Chief of the U.S. Army. Its original purpose was to honor soldiers "who died in defense of their country in the Rebellion" — what we now call the Civil War. ■ In the early days, Decoration Day was a day of patriotism, a day to celebrate the saving of the Union, and to honor the soldiers who gave their lives to preserve it. Soldiers' graves were strewn with flowers, and military groups marched in uniform with the flag proudly displayed. Orators recited Lincoln's Gettysburg Address and the crowds sang patriotic hymns. ■ By 1908, 43 years after the Civil War ended, the ranks of Union veterans were thinning fast — 791 lay in Lakewood Cemetery. ■ Today, thousands of visitors flock to Memorial Day ceremonies at Lakewood to honor fallen soldiers of many wars. A military program sponsored by the Veterans of Foreign Wars and the American Legion is held each year at the Soldiers' Memorial. Other visitors come throughout the day to remember family, friends, and loved ones.

HAIL TO THE HEROES

Commemoration on a large scale occurred every year on Decoration Day, which later became Memorial Day. Established in 1868, the holiday memorialized those who died in the Civil War. Later, Decoration Day became a more generalized occasion, marked by pageantry and patriotism, giving the public the opportunity to commemorate the nation's fallen heroes.

The Decoration Day of 1904 was typical of the era: Representatives of Minneapolis's 13 military posts, veterans' organizations, ladies aid societies, drum and bugle corps, plus clergy, musicians, and singing quartets started the festivities at Lakewood Cemetery. Beginning at 9 a.m., individuals decorated the 671 soldiers' graves; speeches, hymns, prayer, and a reading of the Gettysburg Address followed. A lone bugler playing "Taps" completed the program.

At two o'clock in the afternoon, Minneapolis citizens lining the downtown streets cheered eight military divisions, marching four abreast in full uniform accompanied by mounted police. Cannon fire and a 21-gun salute honored the dead. The parade traveled across the steel bridge at the International Auditorium, near St. Anthony Falls. There a program filled with tribute, prayer, and patriotism ended the day.

Though modern Memorial Day celebrations in Minneapolis lack the pageantry of Decoration Days of old, the holiday is still observed at Lakewood Cemetery. Every Memorial Day, thousands of visitors come to Lakewood to commemorate not only fallen soldiers but also friends and relatives. These holiday visitors are greeted by a colorful landscape in full bloom and an atmosphere of peace and tranquility. The American Legion and the Veterans of Foreign Wars sponsor a Memorial Day program at 10 a.m. at the Soldiers' Memorial, built for those who died in the Spanish-American War and World War I. Throughout the day, which is still Lakewood's most popular, people of all ages stroll around the cemetery enjoying the meticulously prepared gardens and grounds.

In 1948, soldiers stand at attention during a military funeral at the Lakewood Chapel.

AND NOW MY VERSES GIVEN WITH LOVE ARE ETCHED FOREVER UP ABOVE.

    🐦 LOIS C. McPHERSON – 1915-1983

Soon after it was built in 1910, the Lakewood Chapel provided a beautiful funeral sanctuary. Here, a casket surrounded by flowers rests beneath the chapel dome.

JACKS OF ALL TRADES

Burial and commemoration at Lakewood Cemetery are links in a chain of rituals and customs that include body preparation, religious or memorial services, and mourning.

John Werness, who with his older brother George founded Werness Brothers Funeral Home, marks 1922 as the beginning of an association with Lakewood Cemetery lasting nearly 70 years. In the spring of that year, John and his father were hoeing weeds on their farm near Cokato, Minnesota, while George worked the cornfield on a horse-drawn cultivator. They saw the local funeral director walking up the road. "Could I talk to George about a job?" the man asked Mr. Werness. The next day George was working in downtown Cokato at the funeral parlor and John was riding the corn cultivator. John soon followed George to Minneapolis, where, like his brother, he enrolled at the University of Minnesota to study business and mortuary science.

The Werness brothers' chosen profession demanded an extra measure of flexibility, resourcefulness, and tact. Until the mid-1930s, funeral directors had to be prepared for every contingency. The process often began with a phone call at two or three in the morning telling Werness that someone had passed away. "We first asked if we could take the body to the mortuary," Werness says. "Many times the family refused. In that case, we worked in the home, sometimes by kerosene lamp because even then, some homes in Minneapolis didn't have electricity."

Many families didn't have cars either, so Werness often arranged to drive the family to the funeral parlor to select a casket. "Because funerals were often held at home, our main concern then was whether or not we could get the casket inside the house to conduct the service," he says. Church funerals were rare in the 1920s and 1930s, especially in winter, because most churches were not heated during the week.

Though they were common, funeral services at home required extensive and careful planning. For services in town, Werness had to complete a long list of legal requirements and act as liaison with the cemetery and suppliers: He brought folding chairs, a portable organ, a clergyman (if necessary), and a badge to mark the front door. (The badge prevented interruptions in the service by mail carriers or unexpected visitors.) After the service came the procession to the cemetery — often in high style. For the Werness brothers that meant cutaway coats, raised collars, and derby hats.

"Services in the countryside required even more forethought," Werness recalls. "We brought our own lowering device, grass greens — even a shovel and spade because we never knew whether the grave in the country cemetery would be big enough."

By the mid-1930s, Werness was well acquainted with Lakewood Cemetery, enjoying its beauty and its professional commitment. "Lakewood rendered excellent services to funeral directors," he recalls.

At the turn of the century, tradition required that mourners dress in black. In 1900, Mrs. Brown, in full mourning costume, visited her family monument.

WE'LL CATCH THE BROKEN THREADS AGAIN AND FINISH WHAT WE HERE BEGAN —

HEAVEN WILL THE MYSTERIES EXPLAIN AND THEN ⁃ OH THEN WE'LL UNDERSTAND.

❧ ROBERT E. BENNER – 1931-1934

BLACK FOR MOURNING

Traditional funerals were conducted with somber dignity. For many years, Werness wore black formal clothing and was accompanied by mourners dressed in black — which symbolized the solemnity of death and showed their respect for the deceased. Why black? Because prehistoric superstition established it as the appropriate color for mourning.

Until the modern era, people believed that the spirit of the dead could enter and possess the body of a living person. To guard against this, white men painted their bodies black at funerals to disguise themselves from the spirits. The same belief led black African tribes to coat themselves with white chalk.

Black paint evolved into black clothing, which was worn by the relatives of the deceased for weeks, months — even years. In Mediterranean countries, a widow wore black clothing and a veil for a year to hide from her husband's roaming spirit. Following the death of her husband, Prince Albert, in 1861, Queen Victoria of England dressed in black until the day she died — 40 years later. By that time, the superstitions had faded, but the clothing ritual had become of paramount importance in Europe and the United States. Large processions of formally attired mourners wearing top hats and long tails or black gowns showed a person's station in life. Sometimes formal dress was supplied by funeral directors to paid "professional mourners" who accompanied the coffin with a convincing display of sorrow. Cast-off mourning clothes were often purchased cheaply by chimney sweeps, who found the black color ideal for their work. This gave rise to the curious custom of chimney sweeps wearing top hats and long tails.

An estimated 30,000 people turned out to mourn the state's first Farmer-Labor governor, Floyd B. Olson. Two railroad freight cars packed with flowers were sent to adorn his grave at Lakewood Cemetery.

WAITING FOR THE SUN

Before backhoes or other machines existed to dig graves in frozen ground, winter burial in northern climates was nearly impossible. For a premium, Lakewood could burn downed timber or coals on a lot to soften the ground so it could be dug. Most families, however, chose to store their deceased until spring, when burial could be accomplished more easily. For storage purposes, the Lakewood Chapel, built in 1910, included an underground vault with 600 crypts. In any given year, Lakewood stored nearly half of its annual burials there. Though storage is unnecessary at Lakewood today, thanks to a stable of equipment, the cemetery sometimes provides this service for small-town funeral parlors that lack storage facilities or the equipment to open a grave in winter.

GOVERNOR FLOYD B. OLSON (1891-1936)

Floyd B. Olson was born in Minneapolis in 1891 and worked as a stevedore, a miner, and in lumber camps in Canada and Alaska before returning to Minneapolis to study law. After he was admitted to the bar in 1915, Olson quickly became involved in Democratic Party politics, and suffered a number of defeats before he was appointed Hennepin County attorney. ■ Olson's leftist views were too radical for the Democrats, however, and the Democrats were too conservative for him. In the 1920s, Olson joined the progressive Farmer-Labor Party, and was elected the state's first Farmer-Labor governor in 1930. ■ A fearless fighter for equality and social justice, Olson served as governor through the worst years of the Great Depression, from 1931 to 1936. Dealing with a hostile legislature, Olson threatened the state with martial law and the confiscation of wealth to secure the passage of his social relief measures during the Depression years. He also put an end to mortgage foreclosures during that period. ■ In 1934, Olson sided with labor in a major truck drivers' strike and subsequently called out the militia to protect the truckers. Minnesota was under martial law for five weeks. Olson was backed by the Federal Court, which declared martial law better than mob rule. ■ Olson lived and served in a pivotal period of U.S. political history, and his understanding and compassion for the common worker brought much-needed reforms to Minnesota. During his life, workers gained the right to reach collective agreements, farm product prices were adjusted, and unemployment insurance and national retirement pensions were instituted. ■ This difficult political climate, and the long and tiring election campaigns, contributed to a decline in his health. He died in August 1936 — only 44 years old — at the height of his popularity. Olson Memorial Highway is named in his honor.

In 1936, the funeral for Governor Floyd B. Olson, Minnesota's first Farmer-Labor governor, was the largest ever held at Lakewood Cemetery.

In the 1950s, Lakewood still boasted acres of land that were largely untouched.

PARING DOWN THE PACKAGE

A few Lakewood employees can still recall two elderly sisters who visited the cemetery three or four times a week during the 1950s and early 1960s. Dressed in black, the women brought books to read as they sat among the monuments of their family members. Such visitations were common at the turn of the century, but are rare nowadays.

President Ronald A. Gjerde, Jr., who joined the Lakewood staff in the late 1960s, has witnessed this decline in attendance during the past two decades. "We used to see more people here and more frequent visits," he says. "Traditions are changing, for a number of reasons."

In the past, families were large and people stayed in one area. In Minneapolis, as in communities elsewhere, most families remained in their hometown for generations. This was reflected in the options available to those purchasing lots at Lakewood. "When I first came here in 1925, you couldn't buy anything smaller than a four-grave lot," says former Superintendent Paul Anderson. Many families bought much more. Lakewood's largest family lot, purchased in 1963, provided space for the burial of 360 people.

In the last few decades, however, much has changed. Families are smaller; people are more mobile. Children grow up and move away from home, returning only for visits. As a result, Lakewood's policies have also changed. Once Lakewood thought big; now it thinks small. Convenience and service for lot owners and their families is stressed. In addition, the Association is concerned that Lakewood remain available to the public. A rule passed in the 1970s prevents the sale of more than 12 grave spaces to any individual.

The availability of space at Lakewood enabled families to purchase large family lots. Since the 1970s that has changed. Today the cemetery limits the size of a family lot to 12 grave spaces.

FREEDOM OF CHOICE

Changes in society are also evident in a trend toward individual expression in funeral or memorial services. To John Werness, whose career spans more than half a century, the changes are striking. "Years ago, we knew exactly how services would be conducted for Catholic or Protestant funerals. Tradition guided us," he says. "People are freer to do whatever they want today." Gone are the days of veils and long dark clothing. Instead, people now dress more casually. "People wear sports clothes, pants suits, bright clothing. Things have changed considerably," says Werness.

Monuments to children are some of Lakewood's most touching memorials. A monument to Ella Louise Hankenson, who died in 1888 at age five, is found in Section 7.

"We recognize individual values and are more than willing to compromise to please family members," says Ron Gjerde. "We want people to feel they have our support at what is always a difficult time." However, Lakewood is mindful of the need to maintain an air of dignity and decorum in conducting a funeral on the premises, and for that reason, some requests are refused.

THE LONG HAUL

Gjerde embodies another Lakewood tradition — loyalty and longevity. Despite rapid change and high employee turnover elsewhere, Lakewood Cemetery has many employees with a long history of service. A 20-year stint with the organization is commonplace — and some have achieved tenures exceeding half a century. Paul Anderson, superintendent from 1946 to 1972, was 21 when he joined Lakewood in 1925. David Hatlestad, who retired from the presidency in 1989 after nearly 40 years, was two years out of college when he signed on in 1950. Three Lakewood employees — Earl Clark, Roy Nelson, and Emil Erickson — have broken the 50-year mark.

Dedication to the organization is also found among its trustees. Original founder George A. Brackett served on the board for 50 years, as did Robert L. Brooks, Sr., who joined in 1936. Charles M. Loring, another founder, served for 48 years, while Perry Harrison, Russell H. Bennett, Fred B. Snyder, Goodrich Lowry, and John S. Pillsbury, Jr., each served for 35 years or more. Present Lakewood trustee Henry S. Kingman, chairman of the Lakewood board of trustees, best expresses the trustees' commitment: "There are many generations buried here. Lakewood has been a great comfort to many individuals and families, and a great asset to the community in which we live. Such a legacy encourages our continued commitment."

UNDER THE PAGODA

For most of its history, Minnesota has been home to a small but thriving Chinese community. Despite the high cost, Chinese immigrants favored returning the bones of their deceased to China to be buried near ancestors' graves. The practice ended in the 1930s with the Japanese invasion of China. After that, Chinese communities throughout the state organized associations to ensure proper burial for Chinese immigrants. ■ A granite Chinese pagoda-styled monument marks a section in Lakewood Cemetery. Here are buried many of the leaders of Minneapolis's Chinese community. ■ Minneapolis businessman Woo Yee Sing died in 1925. His funeral combined both Christian rites and Chinese traditions. Rather than have his bones returned to China for burial, Woo chose to be buried in Lakewood Cemetery. The funeral service began at Westminster Church in downtown Minneapolis and was followed by a procession that included a Chinese band, which wound its way past the Woo home to collect his soul. Woo's friends and relatives then attended a Chinese dinner, where they paid their respects. The dinner ended with each guest receiving a coin wrapped with a block of sugar "to take away the bitterness."

A granite pagoda marks the location of the Lakewood section reserved for members of Minneapolis's Chinese community.

"She sat like Patience on a monument,

Smiling at grief."

William Shakespeare

Monuments and memorials

Cultures throughout history have created monuments to keep their memories alive. Washington, D.C., is a city of monuments, where millions come to view the statues and temples commemorating America's great people and events. The Vietnam Veterans' Memorial attracts people of all ages who come to honor the dead and to remember.

For more than a century, Lakewood's visitors have enjoyed not only the cemetery's peaceful landscape but also its beautiful monuments. Inspired architecture and meticulously crafted statuary are found throughout the cemetery, particularly in its older sections.

THE WEIGHT OF THE AGES

Like other funeral rituals, the placement of cemetery monuments has origins rooted in the superstitions of Northern Europe. Fearing the dead, families took elaborate precautions to keep the deceased in their graves. A coffin nailed shut provided some security. A large stone on top of the grave gave even greater peace of mind. Those stones, called tombstones, led to the cemetery monuments that today serve as our lasting memorials.

SHE WALKED IN BEAUTY ALL THE DAYS OF HER LIFE. ❧ EFFIE HELENA HAESSLY – 1884-1979

DESIGNING FOR ETERNITY

American cemetery art flourished between 1850 and 1930. During those years, many families bought elaborate and stately monuments to convey their respect for the deceased. Many of these monuments were linked to Greek and Roman themes; others were unique.

In the 19th century, America's most gifted architects — Richard Morris Hunt, Louis Sullivan, Stanford White, Charles F. McKim — and most talented sculptors — Lorado Taft, Daniel Chester French, Augustus St. Gaudens — designed funerary monuments. Their works, and those of lesser-known artists, were listed in tour guides for the nation's major cities.

Until about 1930, architects and sculptors frequently applied their talents to the creation of funerary monuments. Lakewood Cemetery, like other major American cemeteries, is the site of many impressive works of art.

Typically the guide provided a map and a few pages of text for each cemetery. Individual guides to several of the most famous cemeteries were also available and popular. The guide to Mount Auburn, for example, went through more than 20 editions.

Lakewood's cemetery monuments, especially those purchased or commissioned before 1930, show some of the most interesting art and architecture in Minneapolis.

SUPPLY AND DEMAND

At the turn of the century, impressive, ornate monuments were purchased not only by the rich. Middle-class families and even families of modest means erected cemetery monuments that today seem extravagant.

How could these families afford them? Low cost and popular demand helped. In the 1880s and 1890s, an American sculptor earned between $5 and $10 a week, and a hand-carved, life-sized stone figure cost about $40. This was within reach of many American families. High demand also led major department stores to stock cemetery monuments for their mail-order customers.

WHAT'S ART?

At the same time, the appropriateness of monument materials was subject to lively debate within the Lakewood Cemetery Association and the public at large. Most people preferred marble and granite, but others liked the exotic look of bronze and other metals. In November 1889, editorials in Minneapolis newspapers opposed the use of white bronze for cemetery monuments because it was deemed ugly. The Lakewood Cemetery Association joined the chorus of disapproval and shortly thereafter prohibited the erection of white bronze monuments. Today only a few remain.

FUELING AN INDUSTRY

The demand for large cemetery monuments kept the marble quarries of Georgia and the granite quarries of Vermont and Minnesota busy for decades. The rough stone was cut at processing plants and shipped by rail, and later by truck, to dealers throughout the country. Minneapolis monument dealers, who bought top-quality granite and marble from eastern suppliers, also had another source close at hand: Cold Spring Granite, mined near St. Cloud, northwest of the Twin Cities.

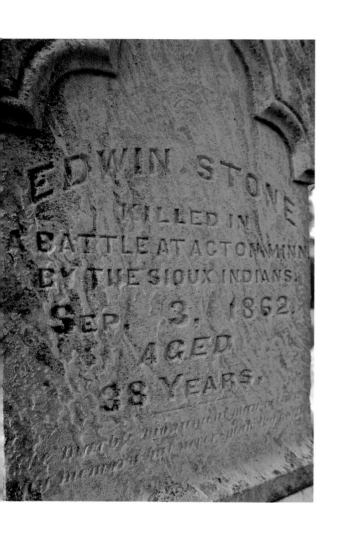

Some Lakewood monuments give a personal glimpse into history. A monument to Edwin Stone, a 38-year-old Minnesota settler, tells that he was killed on September 3, 1862, in the famous Sioux Indian Uprising.

Many families purchased cemetery monuments at the Bogle Monument Company, located near the corner of Hennepin and 36th, across the street from Lakewood. In business for nearly 100 years when it closed in 1989, the company had been the largest monument dealer in the area, and the exclusive supplier of Vermont's Rock of Ages granite, a finely grained, gray stone used in thousands of monuments. Wally Nelson, who owned the Bogle Company, first glimpsed the business from the Lakewood side of the fence.

Like many of its employees, Nelson joined Lakewood right after graduating from high school in 1930. He worked there for 13 years until he was drafted for service in World War II. But instead of returning to Lakewood after the war, Nelson went to work at Bogle's, across the street. Ten years later he bought the company. He ran the sales operation and hired full-time stonecutters to carve, cut, and letter the monuments in the shop. People could select from the 75 to 100 styles on display, or they could direct the company's skilled craftsmen to create a custom-designed monument based on a sketch or a description.

A touching monument to a young member of the Lawrence family is one of Lakewood Cemetery's most unique statues.

Lakewood's Civil War cannon, which stands near the Grand Army of the Republic Memorial, is a tribute to the Union soldiers who fought to preserve the nation. It is the only remaining cannon of its type in the United States.

WAR MEMORIALS

Near the Grand Army of the Republic (G.A.R.) Memorial stands a Civil War cannon with a special history of its own. When it was acquired by Lakewood Cemetery, it bore a plaque claiming that it was forged in England, bought by the Confederate Army, and captured in battle by Union forces. Unfortunately, military historians claim that illustrious tale was fabricated by turn-of-the-century marketing men. ■ Lakewood's Civil War cannon is actually a six-pound Sawyer, a cannon made for the Union Army during the Civil War. Mr. Sawyer, a munitions manufacturer, owned one of scores of companies vying for lucrative government contracts during the war. ■ When the Civil War began, cannonballs were round spheres of a particular weight. To compete more effectively, Sawyer came up with a unique design for his cannon. Rather than shooting a smooth round cannonball, the new cannon used a "mechanical fit" projectile manufactured with grooves in its surface to provide added spin, which improved firing accuracy. ■ This cannon is really a rifle, according to military historian Bernard Paulson, and the Lakewood model is unique. According to Paulson, it is the only existing model of its type remaining in the U.S. ■ Sawyer didn't win a major production contract for a number of reasons. Buying the Sawyer cannon meant that the Army had to buy Sawyer ammunition, which was available only in limited quantities. Second, the cannon's design was not perfected, and it tended to blow up with too much use. However, it was produced in small quantities and used by Union forces in Alabama late in the war. ■ Like most Civil War military hardware, the Sawyer was placed in inventory at one of the many arsenals around the country in the 1880s. At the request of the G.A.R., cannons and other military hardware were donated to G.A.R. posts and Civil War monuments sometime between 1890 and 1910. By 1949, only one Civil War veteran was still living in Minnesota — Albert Woolson, of Duluth, aged 102. With the passing of the last of the veterans, the G.A.R. ceased to exist. ■ Lakewood has other monuments dedicated to the soldiers who have died in our many wars. The Soldiers' Memorial, where Memorial Day services are conducted, is a triptych-style monument to the Civil War, Spanish-American War, and World War I dead. ■ Lakewood is also the final resting place of veterans from even earlier wars, including a couple from the American Revolution, and a few from the War of 1812. ■ Many veterans buried in Lakewood Cemetery have chosen to be remembered for their military service. One was Captain Sidney Hayes. His 12-foot granite monument, with an eagle etched on its face, documents his life: "Born in Louisville, Kentucky, 1880. Answered President McKinley's call for volunteers in 1898 enlisting in Company D, 4th Kentucky volunteer infantry. Captain Hayes served in the Spanish-American War, the Philippine Insurrection, and the Boxer Rebellion in China from 1898 to 1905...Company I, 28th U.S. infantry in 1917 when U.S. entered the World War..."

WHO IN THEIR YOUTH MAINTAINED THE UNION — SO THAT GOVERNMENT OF THE PEOPLE, BY THE PEOPLE, FOR THE PEOPLE, SHALL NOT PERISH FROM THE EARTH.

&❧ THE CIVIL WAR VETERANS OF MINNESOTA – 1861-1865

ETCHED IN STONE

Through the 1920s and 1930s, cemetery monuments were often big, elaborate, and sentimental. Large lots often featured a striking monument, such as a private mausoleum, sarcophagus, or heroic sculpture. Many included flowery poems and epitaphs, declarations of achievement, or tributes to individuals and families.

Monuments from Lakewood's early days are a study in contrasts, reflecting individual style and personality. Some show people as they appeared in life, in statues or portraits. Others contain no information of practical value — merely a nickname; sometimes no name at all.

One Lakewood monument is a life-sized statue of a child, Ella Louise Hankenson, who died in 1888 at the age of five. Her hair in ringlets, Ella gazes out over the grounds, wearing a dress with a lace collar and buttoned shoes.

A bronze relief portrait of Pastor Melchior Falk Gjertsen, donated by the Sons of Norway in 1918, shows a stern and determined man of late middle age, wearing a high collar and wire spectacles.

Unlike monuments of today, many of those erected in the late 19th century identified the deceased by their relationship to the living. For example, a monument to Joseph Nelson, who died in 1886 at the age of 93, bears the simple inscription "Uncle Joe."

Monuments inscribed with the words "Husband," "Wife," "Father," or "Mother" are common. These inscriptions, virtually unheard of today, reveal earlier attitudes toward memorialization. "In many cases, the family did not put the person's name on the marker, because they were primarily concerned with the person's relationship to the living," says Ron Gjerde.

MEMORIALIZING THE HUMAN SPIRIT

Many early monuments were used to commemorate achievements of the deceased. The Pillsbury monument, a towering classical design, has a sheaf of wheat etched on its surface to symbolize the family's leadership in the milling industry. Musical notes are carved in the base of the monument to Emil Oberhoffer, the first conductor of the Minneapolis Symphony.

A monument to Colonel Samuel E. Adams, who lived from 1828 to 1912, is inscribed with a long list of accomplishments: "Paymaster in Civil War, Master State and National Granges, Lieut. Grand Commander, Ancient Accepted Scottish Rite Masons."

The Adams monument also pays tribute to Colonel Adams's wife, Augusta, who served as secretary for the State Grange for 20 years. She died in 1913, at age 79.

Some monuments, like that of Scottish immigrant Joseph Kerr, memorialized at Lakewood, bring a personal connection to great events in American history.

"Born in Scotland, August 9, 1760. Served in the war for American Independence at age of 17 years and in the War of 1812 at age of 52 years. Died in Virginia, July 14, 1843."

Other monuments recount the tragic circumstances of one's death:

"George W. Abraham, Company 9, 1st Regiment Minnesota Volunteers, Died at Andersonville, Georgia, November 12, 1864, Aged 16 years, 9 months."

Monuments to many 19th century families feature beautifully detailed, life-sized statues of women draped in flowing Grecian robes. These grieving female figures, then a popular form of Classical Revival cemetery art, are found in the older sections of Lakewood.

For 27-year-old Eva L. Mackenzie: "Perished from the R.R. [railroad] disaster at Toledo, Ohio, November 28, 1891. She gave her life trying to rescue her two only children."

AMERICAN CLASSICS

Despite minor individual differences and the rare unique memorial,

The Lowry-Goodrich mausoleum, set high on a hill surrounded by majestic oaks, is one of the most impressive examples of Classical Revival funerary architecture in the country. A replica of the Parthenon, the mausoleum is the largest monument in Lakewood Cemetery.

most Lakewood monuments can be classified as one of three popular 19th and early 20th century revival styles — Egyptian, Classical, and Medieval Revival.

The most popular monument style found in American cemeteries and at Lakewood is Classical Revival, which copies the strong simple lines of the ancient Greek or Roman temple and incorporates beautiful carved statuary.

In the 19th century, some Christians criticized this style because of its association with "pagan" culture. Nevertheless, it was a leading choice for European and American families. Many wealthy Americans considered a Classical monument a work of art that linked their names to the cultural enrichment of their communities.

A popular icon of commemoration is the figure of a woman draped in flowing robes. An 1839 guide to Mount Auburn noted that "weeping female figures" adorned a number of family tombs. Seated in grief or gazing skyward, these larger-than-life statues are found throughout Lakewood Cemetery. The Ballard memorial is a good example. It features a grieving woman dressed in a long draping

SHOWMAN'S REST

On the north edge of Lakewood, near the administration building, lies Showman's Rest, a simple granite slab erected by the Midwest Showmen's Association in 1960. The section is the final resting place for clowns, carnival barkers, circus performers, and entertainers of all kinds, many of whom led vagabond lives, without a permanent home. ■ In Showman's Rest is the monument to Callum L. de Villier, who with his partner, Vonnie Kuchinski, danced for 3,780 continuous hours in 1933, setting the world's all-time marathon dance record. They danced at Somerville, Massachusetts, for five months, taking short breaks every hour to use the bathroom or receive medical attention. The partners took turns sleeping, supporting each other. ■ DeVillier met his wife Marjorie at the Fred Astaire Dance Studio at Eighth and Hennepin in the summer of 1939. They were married on Thanksgiving Day, five months later. ■ De Villier's monument features a likeness of him and his partner engaged in a graceful ballroom dance etched into red granite, with the words: "World Champion Marathon Dancer." He lived from 1907 to 1973. ■ DeVillier chose Lakewood because it is close to Lake Calhoun where he and his wife had courted. "We rode around the lake, stopped and talked in the car. It was kind of our home," his widow Marjorie told the *Minneapolis Tribune* in 1981. He designed the monument himself a year before he died. "He was proud of all the hard work he had done for the marathons and thought it should take its place in history," she said.

NO FERRIS WHEEL WITH CIRCLING LIGHTS GLITTERS ACROSS OUR QUIET NIGHTS; BIRD MUSIC HAS REPLACED THE SOUNDS OF BARKERS' CALLS AND MERRY-GO-ROUNDS… WE SHOWMEN WITH OUR FLAGS UNFURLED TOILED TO ADD BRIGHTNESS TO THE WORLD… HOPEFULLY NOW, WITH FRESHENED EYES, WE WAIT GOD'S SHOW, OF PARADISE.

&ederldquo; SHOWMAN'S REST

The monument to marathon dancer Callum de Villier celebrates his life. His monument stands near the Showman's Rest memorial.

garment, sitting at the base of a columned temple. A similar monument, one of the largest at Lakewood, was erected by the Fridley family and features a woman in flowing robes seated beneath an enormous columned arch. And a classical figure of a woman surmounts the massive Walker family monument, erected in 1917 by T. B. Walker, founder of the Walker Art Gallery.

FROM THE LAND OF THE NILE

The easy-to-identify pyramids and obelisks of ancient Egypt constitute another popular monument style. Unlike Greek Classical and Medieval themes, which found expression in buildings of all types, Egyptian motifs were used almost exclusively for cemetery or commemorative art, such as the Washington Monument.

The burgeoning of archeological digs in the late 19th century fueled the

Beginning in the late 19th century, pyramids and obelisks, symbols of ancient Egypt, became popular forms of commemoration in America's cemeteries. In Lakewood Cemetery, the Wood family mausoleum, a tall pyramid constructed in 1905, is one of the most impressive examples.

popularity of the Egyptian style, despite its pagan origins. At Lakewood, the Wood family's private mausoleum, built in 1905, resembles an Egyptian pyramid. Large obelisks memorialize other noted figures at Lakewood, including William H. Dunwoody, a philanthropist who founded the Dunwoody Institute in 1914, and William Henry Eustis, who founded the Dowling School for Crippled Children in 1924.

STURDY VERSUS DELICATE

Medieval Revival monuments, fashioned in hefty, round Romanesque lines or delicate, pointed Gothic shapes, were another popular choice in late 19th and early 20th century America. Relatively few examples of these styles are found at Lakewood.

Romanesque designs were used for a few of the earliest mausoleums, such as those for the Heaton, Vaughan, and Haynes families. Lakewood's original entrance gate and administration building, built in 1888, were also Romanesque in design.

The Gothic style, which reached its full flowering in the medieval cathedrals of Europe, was considered the true architecture of Christianity. The detail and delicacy of this style, however, made it more expensive for monuments than the Classical or Egyptian styles. Three fine examples of Gothic style can be found at Lakewood in the mausoleum for the Mars family and the monuments for the Carlson and Schlampp families.

THE SPIRIT OF WILD AMERICA

Not everyone was enamored with the Egyptian, Classical, or Medieval monument styles. At the turn of the century, Kansas Senator John J. Ingalls wrote: "I hate those obelisks, urns, and stone cottages, and should prefer a great natural rock...one of the great boulders known as the 'last rocks' of the prairie...with a small surface smoothed down, just large enough to make a tablet in which could be inserted the bronze letters of our name...and nothing else."

Many of those buried at Lakewood shared Ingalls's preference for a natural, simple marker. Large glacial boulders, which symbolize America's vast wilderness, rest on a number of lots throughout Lakewood Cemetery, further examples of the varied philosophies and values of many Minneapolis families.

The intricate architectural detail found in many Lakewood monuments was created during the age of American cemetery art, which flourished from 1850 to 1930.

The Minneapolis Fire Department Relief Association monument honors deceased firefighters. Erected in 1892, the monument features a fireman in the dress uniform of that year, which consisted of a long coat and square-billed cap.

ETHNIC SECTIONS

Minneapolis's ethnic diversity is reflected throughout Lakewood. Monuments to Swedish, Norwegian, and German families are interspersed with those to Greek, Hmong, and Chinese families. The lettering on several monuments is carved in alphabets that originated continents away. They bear witness to the immigrants who came to Minnesota but remained tied to the lands of their birth.

Years ago, Lakewood set sections aside for Greek Orthodox and Chinese families wishing to be buried with their countrymen. St. Mary's Greek Orthodox Church reserved one-third of a section for its parishioners, while many members of the Chinese community are laid to rest near a granite pagoda.

Some groups subtly express their ethnicity by choosing a particular monument style rather than a specific location. For example, carving monuments in the shape of a log or a tree trunk, symbolizing a love of the forest, is a frequently used motif among German-Americans, while the graves of Irish-Americans are frequently marked with large Celtic crosses.

TOGETHER IN MEMORY

Several memorials at Lakewood are dedicated to groups. For example, there is the monument to the victims of Minneapolis's worst milling disaster, the Washburn "A" Mill explosion on May 2, 1878, erected by the Minneapolis Head Millers Association. Carvings on the obelisk include a set of millstones and a bevel gear wheel with a broken tooth. The names of the 18 workers are carved on the face of the obelisk.

There is also the Minneapolis Fire Department Relief Association Memorial, erected in 1892. A statue of a fireman in the square-billed cap and dress uniform of the day is surrounded by the graves of firefighters who lost their lives in the line of duty between 1881 and 1979.

A Civil War soldier in a Union uniform stands atop the Grand Army of the Republic Memorial, donated by the Lakewood Cemetery Association in 1889 to honor the Civil War dead.

Best known of all is the Soldiers' Memorial, dedicated to the soldiers of the Civil War, Spanish-American War, and World War I, and site of Lakewood's annual Memorial Day service.

LIBERTY, EQUALITY, FRATERNITY

Kinship through a professional, fraternal, or religious organization provides life's most meaningful association for many people. They acknowledge this bond by choosing to be buried next to their fellows. Tributes to the Society of Friends, the Masons, Elks, Odd Fellows, and the Grange are found on many Lakewood monuments, either collectively, in special sections, or individually.

The most impressive of the fraternal monuments is Elks Rest, a majestic bronze elk standing on a large boulder, partly encircled by scores of members' graves.

ERECTING MONUMENTS

Like much of the building and maintenance work done at Lakewood before the era of hydraulics and combustion engines, the task of installing ceme-

A life-sized bronze elk statue by E. L. Harvey stands on a boulder overlooking the lake and guards the members of the Brotherhood of Paternal Order of Elks, a fraternal organization. Scores of Elks who have died since 1900 are buried in semi-circles around the statue.

In 1907, Minneapolis businessman Louis Rocheleau commissioned a monument in memory of his wife, Charlotte, who died that year at age 37. It is the tallest monument in Lakewood Cemetery.

tery monuments was both challenging and dangerous. Yet this was the time when families chose the largest and most elaborate funerary monuments.

The installation of the tallest monument in Lakewood, commissioned in 1907 by Louis Rocheleau in memory of his wife, Charlotte, was daunting. The monument features a statue of Charlotte, who died at the age of 37, in Grecian robes standing on a huge carved pedestal, holding a single rose in her hand.

The enormous granite monument was shipped to Minneapolis by rail and loaded onto horse-drawn wagons at 28th Street. Lakewood employees still tell the story of how four teams of horses struggled to pull the monument's great granite base to the cemetery. The heaving horses plodded slowly toward the gates, their bellies, the story goes, nearly dragging on the ground.

Once the monument arrived at Lakewood, the cemetery staff faced the formidable task of erecting it on the lot. Men, horses, an elaborate system of ropes and pulleys, and a huge wooden tripod raised the multi-ton monument off the wagons and lowered it into place.

Although putting up a monument was dangerous work, the Rocheleau monument and other large ones like it were installed without major incident. Once, however, ropes supporting a monument snapped, and down came an enormous slab of granite. Luckily no one was hurt, but ever since then Lakewood has contracted the work of erecting monuments to outside firms with specialized modern equipment.

THE END OF AN ERA

Rapid changes in American life after World War II dramatically affected the cemetery business, which had occupied a stable position in society for many decades. Increasing mobility and changing family structures began to alter long-held ideas regarding monuments and commemoration.

Smaller family lots, the increasing cost of labor and materials for traditional monuments, and the decline of a commemorative consciousness gave rise to new concepts about burial.

In 1948, Superintendent Paul Anderson consulted with landscape architect Arthur Nichols and decided to pursue the "no monument" plan for the development of the northeast corner and other new sections of Lakewood. The idea was to save costs and space, and to blend in with the cemetery entrance.

Anderson had all individual grave markers lowered flush to the ground to allow grass cutting with power equipment. The move allowed Lakewood to

The Garden of Faith features a stained-glass monument surrounded by junipers, columnar buckthorn, and euonymus shrubs. It is one of Lakewood's nine memorial park gardens, each distinguished by a central monument.

divert its crew of full-time trimmers to other activities. Other equally dramatic changes soon followed.

THE LAKEWOOD GARDENS

In 1951, Lakewood developed its first memorial park section. Instigated by Paul Anderson and based on a concept that originated in southern California, the new section prohibited the use of traditional, upright monuments. Instead, one central monument depicts each section's theme.

In addition to cutting maintenance costs sharply, the new sections were extremely simple and attractive. The "marble orchard" of monuments that filled the cemetery's older sections now symbolized a bygone era, superseded in these new sections by a sweeping natural landscape, broken only by winding, well-kept roads. "People came into Lakewood and said, 'This looks just like a park,' " Paul Anderson recalls.

Today, Lakewood boasts nine memorial park gardens. Their central monuments cover a range of religious and secular themes, which were created by

WHERE THE LIGHT SHINES BRIGHTEST, THE SHADOWS THERE CUT SHARPEST, BUT, O LORD, LET THY LIGHT BE BRIGHT!

ঌ GARDEN OF MEMORIES SUNDIAL

Lakewood superintendents with the help of the Association trustees, clergy, artists, and monument makers. The Garden of Memories, for example, features a 15-foot sundial and an inscription.

DOUBLE VAULTS SAVE SPACE AND MONEY

The post-World War II era brought other interment options to Lakewood Cemetery. The lawn crypt, initiated in the late 1940s by Fort Lincoln Cemetery in Washington, D.C., offered patrons two interments in a single space by excavating to the depth necessary to accommodate a double vault. The first interment is in the lower chamber, the second in the one above, separated by a concrete shelf.

Lakewood installed its first lawn crypt section in the mid-1960s and now has five lawn crypt gardens.

FOR THE TRADITIONALISTS

By the end of the 1960s, the cemetery lot with a traditional free-standing monument was only one option among many, and the development of new traditional sections has been minimal. Even so, families can still buy lots where they can erect a monument above ground. Lakewood regulates the size, lettering, and placement of the monument on the lot. Markers for individual family members lie flush with the ground.

Although the development of traditional burial lots has been diminishing, the majority of burials conducted at Lakewood today continue to be in traditional lots. "Of the 1,200 burial services we conduct each year, 800 are casket burials placed in traditional grave sites, with the single casket occupying a single space and one marker," says Ron Gjerde. "And of the 800 cremations we conduct every year, in about 200 the cremated remains are placed in a traditional lot."

A soaring obelisk reaches toward the winter sky.

THE FRIDLEYS

Abram M. Fridley, born in 1817, was a frontier agent, a farmer, and a Minnesota State Representative who introduced the first women's suffrage bill in the Minnesota Legislature. Fridley, Minnesota, is named in his honor. Fridley erected an extravagant monument, one of the largest in Lakewood. ■ Fridley's 27-year-old great-granddaughter, Mary Fridley Price, died on November 28, 1914, after a fall from a steep bluff while trying to retrieve her dog near East River Road. Her husband, Fred Price, and his friend, Charles Etchison, were tinkering under the hood of the Prices' 1913 Cadillac touring car, which had stalled on their afternoon drive. ■ Following her death, Fred Price inherited her estate, valued at $23,000, a substantial sum at the time. ■ A year after Mary's death, in October 1915, Price filed a civil suit for $7,500 against the Minneapolis Park Board, alleging negligence in failing to erect a guard rail where Mary fell. In preparing a defense, the Park Board conducted a detailed investigation of the circumstances of her death. On the stand, a Park Board expert revealed that Mary's body was found 42 feet below and 27 feet beyond the outermost cliff edge. The expert testified that some propulsion, not a mere fall, would have been necessary to bring her to that location, since she weighed less than 100 pounds. Midway through the trial, Price abruptly dismissed his lawsuit. ■ Price's greed was his undoing. Suddenly suspicious of his former son-in-law, Mary's father, David Fridley, retained former police detective and private investigator John P. Hoy to investigate the case. It is believed that Hoy was the first private detective to take on an important murder case in Minnesota. Hoy quickly discovered that Price had never legally divorced his first wife, and he had been living with another woman since the night of Mary's death. Further investigation brought an indictment for first-degree murder against Fred Price on December 1, 1915. Price's accomplice, Charles Etchison, then confessed to authorities that he had witnessed the murder, and testified against Price in a jam-packed courtroom at a publicized trial. ■ Price was convicted of first-degree murder on January 15, 1916, and sentenced to life in prison. He died in prison and was cremated at Lakewood Cemetery in 1930.

Book in hand, a thoughtful, classically draped woman sits beneath a towering arch of the Fridley monument, one of the largest in Lakewood Cemetery.

"He builded better than he knew
The conscious stone to beauty grew."

Ralph Waldo Emerson

ARTISTRY IN ARCHITECTURE

The history of a city can be read in its architecture. Houses and public buildings are at first merely evidence that a community exists. Soon, however, the city's architecture begins to represent shared ideals, visions, and collective pride. One day, if luck and hard work prevail, a city's buildings — New York's Empire State Building, the Sears Tower in Chicago — inspire awe, symbolizing the city's greatness.

The history of Lakewood is similarly linked to its architectural achievements. Paralleling the growth of Minneapolis, Lakewood's early structures were later replaced with buildings of brilliance and enduring beauty.

In 1888, more than 15 years after its founding, Lakewood Cemetery constructed an impressive red granite reception house complete with turrets and a broad arched gate to shelter carriages from the elements. The building housed the cemetery's administrative offices until 1930, when the present Administration Building was completed and the existing structure was dismantled.

A TASTEFUL NEW BUILDING

In 1880, the *Minneapolis Star Journal* reported that the Lakewood Cemetery Association planned to build a reception house, entrance gate, and 2,500-foot fence along 36th Street. However, the project was delayed for more than seven years, for reasons lost to time. Construction finally began in the spring of 1887 and in 1888 the reception building and entrance gate were completed at Hennepin Avenue for $51,000.

Lakewood's new gate was a magnificent Romanesque arch, built of red granite and set back at an angle 50 feet from 36th Street. Designed by architect Frank I. Read, the entry was decorated with inlays of stone and brick and representations of the lotus flower, the cross, love birds, olive branches, and passionflowers.

Attached to the arch, the Reception House was built in the same imposing Romanesque style. Its entrance resembled entrances to many Minneapolis homes of the time. Though the Reception House was a large, stately building, it consisted of only two rooms, one for receptions, the other an office for the superintendent.

In 1893, when Lakewood Cemetery hosted the seventh annual convention of the American Association of Cemetery Superintendents, the visitors found "an imposing granite structure with its offices, the commodious receiving tomb, and chapel." Visiting cemetery superintendent John G. Barker of Boston was much impressed: "We find the entrance at once beautiful and pleasant, and the tasteful manner in which it is constructed and arranged gives all who go there a cordial welcome."

As Lakewood grew, the Association expanded public access to the cemetery on the east and west with a new gate at 40th Street and another near the Lake Calhoun streetcar stop.

In 1906, the Association added a Public Comfort Building at the Lake Calhoun streetcar entrance to the cemetery. The small, rounded, stone structure of Romanesque design faced the lake and was occupied by a female attendant, who greeted guests at the west entrance and helped ladies dust off and freshen up for their visit to the cemetery. The Lake Calhoun Rest House, as it came to be known, was razed in the 1950s.

MORE THINGS ARE WROUGHT BY PRAYER THAN THIS WORLD DREAMS OF.

• ALFRED, LORD TENNYSON
    PRAYING HANDS MONUMENT

In 1906, Lakewood constructed a Public Comfort Building at the Lake Calhoun streetcar stop on the west side of the cemetery. A female attendant employed by the Association greeted cemetery visitors and helped ladies freshen up for their visit to Lakewood.

RAISE THE NEW, RAZE THE OLD

By 1926 the original administration building had become inadequate to meet the needs of the staff and public. Paul Anderson, who joined the Lakewood staff the year before, recalls the building's deficiencies: "There was no privacy for visitors, not even a place to sit down. Only a counter separated visitors from the office staff. We'd often have to stand there talking to a widow on what was probably the worst day of her life, within hearing and sight of the other staffers."

To solicit designs for a new building and entrance gate, the Lakewood Board offered $500 to each architect who submitted drawings and plans. Architects Harry Wild Jones, Hewitt and Brown, Kees and Bowstead, Magney and Tusler, and Ernest Kennedy responded to the request. In 1928, after he presented his plan and model, Lakewood retained Minneapolis architect Ernest Kennedy, at a projected total cost of $348,326.

Kennedy planned a classical Greek structure, featuring a symmetrical eight-columned facade positioned 250 feet from 36th Street and Hennepin Avenue. The one-story building, 87 feet wide by 138 feet long, was designed to house

administrative and private offices, conference rooms, storage facilities, and a floral shop, which would connect the new building to the existing greenhouses and offer visitors a convenient way to buy flowers.

Kennedy positioned the new gates closer to 36th Street than the original building and entrance, so that the existing Reception House could remain undisturbed until the new building was completed.

When the new Administration Building was completed in 1930, cemetery visitors were greeted in a spacious administrative office decorated in marble and ornamental bronze.

Once the details were worked out, only the choice of building materials remained. Kennedy toured the region to inspect buildings constructed of tooled granite or Indiana limestone, the two materials originally proposed in his plan. He traveled throughout Minnesota and as far south as Iowa City, Iowa, before he made his choice of high-grade Cold Spring pearly gray granite. The decision made, the J. and W. A. Elliott Company, general contractors, went to work under Kennedy's supervision.

Similarly fine materials and the same attention to detail were used in the building's interior. The main stairs, with their ornamented iron railings, and the walls and cornices of the vestibule, lobby, and stairways, were made of light Botticini marble. Darker Botticini marble framed the doorways while the floors were of Tennessee marble with a violet Formosa border and central design. The superintendent's office featured walls of rich walnut paneling with holly wood inlays and a floor of wide oak boards. The double entrance doors were of ornamental bronze, used also in the window grilles.

Two eight-and-a-half-foot-high columns flanking Lakewood's main entrance were constructed of the same pearly gray granite as the building's exterior. Three panels depicting "Light," "Darkness," and "Peace" in cast bronze relief accented the attached bronze gates.

The new Administration Building was completed in 1930 at a cost close to the original bid.

The original Reception House was razed after the offices were moved, a process vividly remembered by Wally Nelson, who joined the office staff in January 1930. He and the other office employees worked several nights one week to haul 60 years of accumulated records from the old office to the safe in the new building.

The Administration Building remained untouched until 1977, when the Association gave the interior a facelift — repainting and redecorating, installing improved lighting, and adding an employee lunchroom. A major remodeling project in 1992 brought the Administration Building up to date.

FENCES

In about 1910, Lakewood acquired the remainder of the Saunders Park neighborhood and removed the houses and streets. But most of the area remained open and undeveloped, stretching out like a large park dotted with elms. People traveling east along 36th Street who wanted to turn south on Dupont began to cut

When it opened in 1930, the spacious new Administration Building included private conference rooms for Lakewood visitors.

a dirt path diagonally across Lakewood's property. Superintendent Arthur Hobert was not pleased and decided to put a stop to it.

Hobert ordered the grounds workers to install a barbed-wire fence that blocked the shortcut and forced drivers of horse-drawn carriages and sputtering cars back onto the public roads.

The next day, a fire in south Minneapolis brought firefighters racing toward the blaze in horse-drawn wagons. To save time, they shot down the Lakewood shortcut, the horses thundering over the well-worn path. They saw the fence, but it was too late to stop. The firemen weren't injured, but the horses were cut and bleeding, wrapped in barbed wire. It was a painful lesson for all. From then on, travelers kept to the road.

Though prominent and long-standing, Lakewood's entrance gates have also been the site of accidents. Despite a heavy iron cable stretched across the entrance, the gate has often taken a beating from reckless drivers roaring up Hennepin Avenue.

Some of the damage to the gate has been intentional. Only a year after its construction, the gate was torn off its hinges and twisted out of shape by a group of "noisy and boisterous men and women," which compelled the Association to offer a $100 reward for information leading to their arrest.

Between 1947 and 1952, the entrance was redesigned. The broad bronze-paneled gates were removed from the main entrance and a large garden was centered in front with openings on either side. Curbs were extended past the greenhouse on the left and to the chapel on the right.

The heavy wrought iron fence that now encloses the entire cemetery was installed during the Depression. With this purchase, Lakewood boosted a local iron company's revenues by $25,000. "They were hanging on by their teeth," says Paul Anderson, "and we helped them out." The fence finally provided the safety and security the Association was looking for.

The fence is a formidable obstacle, consisting of 345 sections, each 16 feet long and about 6 feet high with pilings two inches thick. Painting the fence was quite an undertaking and so was insuring it. Former President David Hatlestad remembers a 1975 discussion with an insurance agent: "A 16-foot section cost about $2,000 to replace, and the agent wanted us to count every section, so I sent someone out. When the sections were tallied, the agent multiplied the number by $2,000, and told me he was basing the premium on the total — almost $700,000."

THE MIDNIGHT STARS ARE GLEAMING
ON A LONE AND SILENT GRAVE,
BENEATH SLEEPS ONE WE LOVE,
BUT ONE WE COULD NOT SAVE.
HIS WEARY HOURS, HIS DAYS OF PAIN,
HIS WEARY NIGHTS ARE PASSED.
HIS EVER-PATIENT, WORN-OUT FRAME
HAS FOUND SWEET REST AT LAST.
&. BENJAMIN F. GATES –
APRIL 18, 1857-FEB. 6, 1919

The agent had a head for figures, but not much common sense. Hatlestad set him straight: "You think the whole fence is going to go down all at once!"

"I think he was looking for a bigger premium," Hatlestad concludes.

COMPANY HOUSING

Lakewood Cemetery was several miles from town in its earliest days, and people came by horse, carriage, and then the streetcar, once it was installed in the 1880s. Commuting long distances to work every day was uncommon and impracticable — roads were rough and transportation was slow. These factors, along with a 10-hour work day, forced most people to live close to their jobs.

Beginning in 1894, the Lakewood Cemetery Association provided homes such as this for Lakewood superintendents across the street from the cemetery's main entrance. The Association also provided homes for some laborers on the cemetery grounds.

In 1880, the Association bought 2½ acres facing the cemetery on 36th Street for construction of a superintendent's house, a house for laborers, and a stable. But these ambitious plans were stalled by lack of funds. Finally, in 1894, local contractors Leck and McLeod completed a two-story, five-bedroom frame house for the Lakewood superintendent at a cost of $3,059.

When Paul Anderson became superintendent in 1946, he decided to build equity in a home of his own. Shortly afterward, Lakewood sold the house at 1412 W. 36th Street for $10,500. The remodeled structure is now called Vail Place.

Lakewood houses at 1404 and 1009 W. 36th Street and at 3537 Hennepin Avenue South provided commute-free housing for Lakewood's employees over several decades. Another Lakewood house, with a huge attached barn and garage, was built inside the cemetery near the 36th Street entrance. For many years it was home to Lakewood's live-in caretaker, usually the grounds superintendent, who opened and closed the gates and kept an eye on the horses. Grounds superintendent Roy Nelson lived there until the 1940s when he bought his own home. Employee Elmer Lundquist followed Nelson. The last Lakewood employee to live on the grounds was Ray Lindmark, who, after retiring, left Minneapolis in the early 1970s. The building was demolished in the mid-1970s. The city had long since surrounded Lakewood, and commuting to work has become the norm rather than the exception.

HARRY WILD JONES (1859-1935)

Architect Harry Wild Jones, designer of the Lakewood Chapel, was born in Michigan on June 9, 1859. His was a family of patriots — his grandfather was noted as the composer of "My Country 'Tis of Thee."
■ Jones attended a private prep school in Rhode Island. He earned a B.A. from Brown University and a degree in architecture from Massachusetts Institute of Technology. He worked with architect H. H. Richardson in Boston before going to Europe to study French and Italian architecture. Jones moved to Minnesota in 1884, and set up an office. Three years later he built a home in the country, now 5101 Nicollet Avenue South. ■ In addition to the Lakewood Chapel, Jones designed many other Minneapolis structures, including the old Cream of Wheat Building, the entrance building of the Nicollet Baseball Park, the first Lake Harriet Pavilion, all gone; and Butler Square, the Washburn Water Tower, Calvary Baptist Church at 2608 Blaisdell, the Scottish Rite Temple at 2011 Dupont Avenue South, and a number of homes in the Kenwood neighborhood. Jones was the first professor of architecture at the University of Minnesota.

Prominent Minneapolis architect Harry Wild Jones modeled the Lakewood Chapel after the Haghia Sophia, a temple built in Constantinople by Byzantine Emperor Justinian I, in 537 A.D.

The Lakewood Chapel entrance includes double doors of solid bronze, embellished with ancient religious symbols and capped with a stained-glass transom in the Art Nouveau style. The plaque on the left declares that the building is on the National Register of Historic Places.

THE LAKEWOOD CHAPEL

The beautiful chapel that is the centerpiece of Lakewood Cemetery is the third building on the grounds to be used for the religious ritual of funeral services. A cemetery chapel was a necessity and priority at Lakewood from its earliest days. A temporary wooden chapel, built shortly after Lakewood's founding, was replaced by a modest stone structure near the original reception house a few years later. But a permanent chapel remained a long-term goal.

In 1904, the Association began to solicit preliminary sketches for a new chapel, but other duties and responsibilities slowed the project to a halt. Then in 1906, a group of Minneapolis funeral directors petitioned the Association for action on a new Lakewood chapel.

Shortly afterward, trustees George A. Brackett, C. G. Goodrich, and Cavour Langdon formed a committee to guide chapel development and solicit design concepts from leading architects. At Thomas Lowry's request, the committee agreed to include a crematory in the chapel design.

In March 1908, the Lakewood Building Committee selected Harry Wild Jones, a prominent Minneapolis architect, to design the chapel. Jones had received his degree from MIT and had spent several years in Europe studying French and Italian architecture before settling in Minneapolis in 1884. His knowledge of historical architecture undoubtedly influenced his vision of the Lakewood Chapel.

Jones's winning design was modeled after the Haghia Sophia, an architectural masterpiece of Byzantine Romanesque style built in 537 A.D. by Emperor Justinian I in what is now Istanbul. Jones planned a modified cruciform structure with a large center dome flanked by square towers and smaller domed caps on each corner. While blending well with the landscape, the Romanesque style would complement the existing entrance gate and reception house. The trustees found the design ideal.

In June 1908, the Association selected general contractors Pike and Cook from among six companies bidding for the construction contract. The winning bid was $59,440; construction began in August.

CONSTRUCTION BEGINS

Instead of building the chapel in one phase, Jones agreed to construct it in parts, beginning with the crematory and columbarium (a vault with niches for

SHE LIVED AND BROUGHT UNTO THIS EARTH A BIT OF BEAUTY, LOVE, AND FAITH — AND NOW HER LIFE WILL EVER BE REFLECTED IN YOUR HEART.

&. PETRA C. DICKEY – 1874-1977

The chapel dome is 65 feet high and ringed with 24 stained-glass windows of Art Nouveau design that serve as a sundial, telling the time of day and season. The 12 mosaic angels that also adorn the dome are wrought with religious symbolism.

urns containing the cremated remains of the dead). First, however, under the direction and at the expense of the Lakewood Board of Trustees, Jones traveled west to research crematories and columbariums in Portland, Seattle, San Francisco, Los Angeles, and Denver. Eventually, James Currie, a specialist in columbarium construction, was brought in from Milwaukee to supervise construction, and it was completed in February 1909. Cremation experts from Chicago conducted the first four cremations in the new facility and declared it perfectly sound.

TILL I WALTZ AGAIN WITH YOU. ❧ ALICE J. KUNITZ – MARCH 18, 1907-NOV. 8, 1987

HUNG FROM HEAVEN

The trustees insisted on quality. They supported Jones's preference for building materials of the highest durability and beauty; every detail of the chapel reflects this overriding concern. For example, the double-door entrance was con-

structed of solid bronze and embellished with ancient religious signs: Alpha and omega symbolize the beginning and the end; an Alisy Paty cross represents the four evangelists; and a peacock symbolizes the resurrection and immortality. The doors are capped with a brilliant stained-glass transom in the Art Nouveau style. Other exterior doors, window frames, and sashes are made of copper. The chapel's 65-foot-high, seemingly freestanding dome gives the viewer a sense of awe and airy majesty.

The 24 stained-glass windows circling the dome are also in the Art Nouveau style. The windows, set in metal, serve as a sundial, telling the time of day and the season. The chapel's exterior walls are constructed of reddish-gray St. Cloud granite. The dome and roof were built of Gustavino tile with an outer roofing of Spanish roll tile embedded in elastic cement.

In addition to the domed chapel area, the building design included a retiring room for ladies, a robing space for clergy, and a private chamber for the

New York designer Charles R. Lamb modeled the Lakewood Chapel's interior after the mosaic design of the San Marco Cathedral of Venice. To complete the work, he traveled to the Vatican in Rome to enlist the services of six of Italy's most skilled mosaic artists.

The chapel's interior consists of more than 10 million individual mosaic tessellae, made of marble, colored stone, and glass fused with gold or silver. The design was rendered in Venice and shipped to Minneapolis in 1909.

family of the deceased. The secluded seating area north of the altar offers a family complete privacy and an unobstructed view of the clergy conducting the funeral service.

Designed to seat approximately 200 people, the chapel projects sound as skillfully as it captures light. The acoustics are so nearly perfect that speakers at the rostrum can be heard clearly throughout the chapel, eliminating the need for microphones.

Neither wood nor nails, varnish nor paint was used in the construction of the chapel, making it virtually fireproof. This was a great consolation to the trustees, who were concerned about the fire risk posed by the crematory in the basement.

THE METAMORPHOSIS

Seen from the outside during the construction period, the Lakewood

Chapel was both beautiful and intriguing, its Byzantine flavor enhanced by the artful combination of bronze, tile, and stone. But the unfinished interior had the general ambiance and appearance of a railroad station.

Building Committee Chairman George Brackett recognized that the interior design needed to be absolutely perfect. He appealed to firms nationwide for designs and several responded, including J & R Lamb Studios, a prominent New York company under the direction of Charles R. Lamb. Lamb suggested a Byzantine mosaic design based on the interior of the San Marco Cathedral in Venice. The design incorporated a dazzling display of color and detail into the chapel's overall architectural style. The Board of Trustees soon commissioned Lamb to complete the chapel's interior at a cost of $25,000.

THE MOSAIC MAKERS

Under Lamb's direction, an artisan from Lamb Studios carefully laid out the interior's design on a flat surface, then built molds corresponding to the walls and curves of the chapel.

Few living artists possessed the creativity and skill to realize Lamb's vision, but Lamb knew where to find them. Traveling to Rome, Lamb enlisted the services of six of Italy's most highly accomplished mosaic artists. In Venice, the group began work on the mosaics by creating more than 10 million pieces, called tessellae, from marble, colored stone, and glass fused with gold or silver. No larger than a fingernail, each tile was attached to gummed cloth and shipped to Minneapolis. The artists themselves arrived in the summer of 1909, and painstakingly assembled the masterpiece inside the chapel.

THE MOST PERFECT EXAMPLE

Completed, the chapel interior was a breathtaking work of art and religious symbolism. Four large mosaic figures representing Faith, Hope, Memory, and Love adorn the side walls. The exquisitely detailed figures are based on drawings by Ella Condie Lamb, a noted portrait artist and wife of Charles Lamb.

Twelve angels appear in the chapel dome, relating to the Old Testament's 12 sons of Jacob, 12 tribes of Israel, and 12 gates to the Holy City, and to the 12 disciples of Christ in the New Testament. Positioned at the four points of the compass, four angels holding red roses symbolize "the four corners of the Earth" (Revelations 7:1). The fully extended wings of the angels symbolize their protective spirit.

"UNTIL THE DAY BREAK AND THE SHADOWS FLEE AWAY."

❧ SONG OF SOLOMON 4:6
LAKEWOOD MEMORIAL CHAPEL

The 12 angels circling the chapel dome represent the Old Testament's 12 sons of Jacob, 12 tribes of Israel, and the 12 gates to the Holy City, and the New Testament's 12 disciples of Christ. The angels' gowns also have symbolic meaning. The yellow, or pale, gowns (upper left, lower right) signify death; the blue gown (upper right) symbolizes the resurrection; and the red gown (lower left) stands for life.

The angels wear yellow (called pale), red, and blue gowns. Pale stands for death, red means life, and blue represents the resurrection. The angels have no visible feet because, according to lore, they fly and never touch earth.

In the alcove behind the rostrum, at the far end of the chapel, the mosaics portray entwined olive trees (olives are famous for their healing properties). The changing colors in the leaves represent the cycle of life from spring to winter; the mosaic sky behind the trees is graduated from daytime to nighttime to subtly emphasize the same theme. Below stand the pulpit and a chair, both of carved white Grecian marble and inlaid with gold and blue mosaics.

When all the expenses were tallied, the total cost of the chapel came to $150,000, a large sum in 1910. But the structure's artistry and beauty, and the pride and awe it engendered, far outweighed its price. The Board of Trustees, the Lakewood staff, and the public responded to the new chapel with tremendous enthusiasm.

At the dedication on November 22, 1910, five of Lakewood's original nine trustees were still on the board. In his address, Board President W. D. Washburn spoke proudly of the chapel's "exceptional beauty and magnificence," so fitting to the natural beauty of Lakewood. Artist and architect Charles Lamb spoke eloquently of "Faith," "Hope," "Love," and "Memory," as symbolized in the chapel and our lives: "Religion, if it means anything, is not a hopeless form; religion means a spiritual uplifting, and if we place faith on one side and hope before us, and follow with love, we add a fourth dimension of memory, because enshrined in your hearts and mind must always be the memory of those we have lost."

At the time of its completion, the Lakewood Memorial Chapel was the only building in the United States with an authentic mosaic interior. Visitors often remarked at finding such an outstanding architectural jewel in the heart of the American Midwest. "If this chapel were somewhere in Europe, thousands of Americans would visit it each year," wrote one journalist in a 1931 review. "Never have we seen anything to equal it in this country — not even the famous mosaics of the Library of Congress at Washington impressed us so greatly."

Today, the Lakewood Chapel remains the most perfect example of Byzantine mosaic art in the United States. Many experts believe that a work of such magnitude could not be re-created at any price today — artisans possessing the necessary skills are no longer alive.

TO LIVE IN HEARTS WE LEAVE BEHIND IS NOT TO DIE.

    ❧ SUSANNA P. HAMILTON –
        AUG. 17, 1868-JAN. 21, 1947
        ARTHUR S. HAMILTON, M.D. –
        NOV. 28, 1872-JUNE 2, 1940

The Lakewood Chapel stands today virtually unchanged, with the exception of repairs and minor additions: In 1937, a beautiful Skinner pipe organ brought music to chapel services; a vestibule was added in 1938, and the following year the Flour City Ornamental Iron Company installed new entrance doors, railings, and vases. In 1987, substantial repairs were made to the chapel, and the mosaics and clerestory windows were restored by old world craftsmen. The cost of this latest restoration was more than two and a half times the original cost of the building.

On October 20, 1983, the Lakewood Chapel was added to the National Register of Historic Places, joining other Minneapolis landmarks. Lakewood offers tours of the chapel during regular cemetery hours to individuals and groups interested in the chapel's history and unique beauty.

MAUSOLEUMS: OLD AND NEW

The world's first mausoleum, a combined sepulcher and monument, was built in ancient Greece about 353 B.C., when Artimisia, Queen of Caria, ordered a sumptuous sepulcher erected in honor of her husband, King Mausolus.

The concept of the community mausoleum, the funereal equivalent of the apartment building, first came into vogue in the United States in the early 20th century.

American mausoleums built before the Great Depression often emulated Greek, Egyptian, Gothic, or Romanesque styles and often matched (in terms of size) large public buildings, with grand entrances and lavish sculptures.

THE LAKEWOOD MAUSOLEUM AND COLUMBARIUM

Lakewood delayed building a mausoleum until the spring of 1960, when the Association began to plan the development of a combined mausoleum, columbarium, and garden crypt. The facility would offer year-long visitation, eliminating concerns about inclement weather, and would provide an additional burial option. The Association first consulted with noted mausoleum architect Victor Gilbertson, of Hayes, Gilbertson and Fisher, who recommended the site facing the chapel. Next, the Lakewood Building and Grounds Committee and Superintendent Paul Anderson collected sketches and plans for the project from architectural firms in Minneapolis, Detroit, and New York, then inspected the Queen of Heavens Cemetery mausoleum in Chicago to gather first-hand information.

MY PEACE I GIVE UNTO YOU.

ﻉ FLOYD A. FREDLUND –
1905-1989

Four mosaic figures representing Love, Faith, Memory, and Hope (clockwise, from upper left) adorn the side walls beneath the chapel dome. The figures were based on watercolor renderings by noted portrait artist Ella Condie Lamb, wife of chapel designer Charles Lamb.

Eventually, the Lakewood committee selected the Detroit firm of Harley, Ellington, Corwin and Stirton to complete the design. Watson Construction Company, bidding $1,791,000, won the contract in November 1964 to build the mausoleum. Ground clearing began in November 1965.

In his announcement to the press, Lakewood Board President Robert L. Brooks, Sr. emphasized that preserving space and lowering burial costs were the major factors that led to the decision, along with Lakewood's desire to remain competitive and to satisfy customers. "The mausoleum will prolong the life of the cemetery, no question of that," Brooks told the *Minneapolis Tribune*, "but we're not doing this because of lack of space. We want to modernize like other cemeteries."

A SANCTUARY FOR THE FUTURE

The 14,400-square-foot structure would occupy almost five acres and provide space for more than 3,000 crypts and 2,000 niches. An adjacent fountain and pool, named the Pool of Reflections, linked the mausoleum with the chapel area and would accommodate 1,100 outdoor garden crypts.

In 1965, Lakewood began construction of a 14,400-square-foot mausoleum and columbarium, which would preserve limited cemetery space and expand the funerary options available to the public.

Completed in 1967, the Memorial Community Mausoleum is a modern building made of Minnesota granite, steel, and bronze, decorated with Italian marble, crystal chandeliers, and Impressionist paintings, and furnished with plush carpets and comfortable furniture. A mahogany-paneled chapel is enclosed by stained-glass windows, the work of Willet Stain Glass Studios, a Philadelphia firm that created all of the mausoleum's 24 eight-foot-high stained-glass windows. Illustrating poetry and Bible verses, the windows cast shimmering light throughout the spacious interior.

Seven columbarium rooms within the mausoleum contain individual and family niches for cremated remains. Six rooms are located on the garden level and the seventh is on the second floor.

The rest of the mausoleum houses the crypts: single crypts, side companion crypts, end companion crypts, and Westminster crypts designed to be set below the floor. All are located within the corridors of the building or within semi-private alcoves or sanctuary areas.

The Minneapolis branch of the Daughters of the American Revolution, shown here in 1923, gathered in Lakewood Cemetery three years earlier to honor Minnesota's earliest women pioneers, Attai Lovejoy and Laura Herrick.

PIONEER WOMEN

In 1920, the Daughters of the American Revolution visited Lakewood Cemetery to pay tribute to two of the city's earliest women pioneers. All the children of the city were invited to attend the unveiling of bronze tablets honoring Mrs. Attai Lovejoy and Mrs. Laura Herrick, whose fathers fought the British in the Revolutionary War. ■ Mrs. Lovejoy was born in Amherst, New Hampshire, on October 8, 1780, seven years before the American Constitution was signed, and in what was considered the hardest year of the Revolutionary War. Her maiden name was also Lovejoy and her father, John Lovejoy, fought in the Revolution. She made the long and arduous trip to Minneapolis in 1854 with her husband, William, her son and his wife, and her grandson and his wife. She was 74 years old when she arrived. The Daughters of the American Revolution believed that Attai Lovejoy was born earlier than any other woman who has lived and died in Minneapolis. ■ The second pioneer honored in the 1920 ceremony was Laura Herrick, born Laura Small in Amherst, New Hampshire, in 1810. She married in 1830, moved west to Iowa, and finally settled in Minnesota in 1858 with her husband, Nathan, and their children. She spent her remaining years in Minneapolis, and died at the age of 88. ■ Granite tablets marking the two graves were placed by Genevieve Greaves, the great-great-great-granddaughter of Attai Lovejoy, and Margaret Herrick, the great-granddaughter of Laura Herrick.

When the mausoleum opened in 1967, Lakewood offered a small number of private family rooms, but only two were sold. The practice was discontinued in the 1970s because the area occupied by one of those families alone could serve 150 families choosing columbarium niches. By the mid-1980s, more than half of the available space had been sold.

Today, the Lakewood Memorial Community Mausoleum and Columbarium provides visitors a warm and comfortable haven against the Minnesota elements. Though only names and dates memorialize loved ones on the marble walls of the crypts and niches, tables throughout the building hold flowers and notes from friends and relatives. In some ways, then, with the bright flowers and stained glass, it is always springtime in this spot at Lakewood.

The Pool of Reflections, flanked by trees and gardens, links the Lakewood Memorial Community Mausoleum and Columbarium with the Lakewood Chapel to the east.

The morning sun illuminates the brilliant stained-glass windows of the Lakewood Memorial Community Mausoleum and Columbarium. The windows, created by Willet Stain Glass Studios of Philadelphia, depict a number of spiritual and secular themes.

"Enough, if something from our hands have power

To live, and act, and serve the future hour."

William Wordsworth

FOUNDATION FOR THE FUTURE

Lakewood Cemetery is governed by a Board of Trustees, many of whom are descendants of the cemetery's founders. The Board members are: (seated, left to right) Ronald A. Gjerde, Jr., President, Henry S. Kingman, Jr., Chairman, Russell M. Bennett II, E. Peter Gillette, Jr., (second row) Henry Doerr, Jane West, Stephen P. Duffy, Jr., Helen S. Johnson, Edward (Ned) Dayton, (third row) David T. Bennett, James W. Nelson, Christine A. Morrison, David P. Crosby, (not pictured) Margaret Ankeny, C. Angus Wurtele.

To its founders and the Minneapolis community in the 1870s, Lakewood Cemetery was a public institution similar to schools, libraries, and other service organizations created to meet public needs. The founders considered themselves guardians of the public trust and gave generously of their time and expertise to guarantee the Association's success. They structured its management and operation in accordance with their own successful business practices, with one major exception: They prohibited personal profit.

The original 1874 bylaws established Lakewood Cemetery for the benefit of the community as a non-profit and non-sectarian association. Though the bylaws have been amended or expanded during the past 120 years, the intent of Lakewood's original charter remains unchanged.

THE DECISION MAKERS

A month after its dedication in 1872, Lakewood's founders called a stockholders' meeting to elect the Board of Trustees. These stockholders, called Associates, included the founders and the lot owners, who were entitled to vote in the annual election of trustees. Despite the democratic structure, the annual vote continued to place the cemetery's leadership firmly in the hands of the founders.

As the number of Lakewood lot owners grew, their direct participation in the cemetery's affairs became cumbersome. The Association revised its original bylaws. A self-perpetuating group of 15 Associates was empowered to elect from its membership the nine-member board of trustees who managed the cemetery. Succeeding trustees were chosen from among the six remaining Associates.

For more than a century, the Lakewood Association and the Board of Trustees were composed of men, all leaders in the community. Women were first considered for membership in 1974. The following year, largely through the insistence of Lakewood Trustee Henry S. Kingman, Ruth Leslie Bean was elected the first woman Associate.

More than a century of dedication and commitment by Lakewood's Board of Trustees has helped to create a cemetery of unrivaled beauty and financial stability.

Today, the Lakewood governing body remains a two-tier system of six Associates and nine trustees who represent cemetery lot owners. Many of the trustees are the second or third generation of their families to be involved. Deep family ties and long familiarity with the organization have inspired dedication and interest in the cemetery's management that transcends generations.

"In the old days, when you became a trustee for an organization, it was for life," says Lakewood Trustee Russell M. Bennett II. Currently, Lakewood Associates and members of the Board remain active until age 72; officers retire at age 70. Retirement doesn't necessarily end participation in the Association, however. "That kind of dedication has made Lakewood successful," says former President David Hatlestad. Said Benton Case, a trustee from 1963 to 1976 who was known for his gentle humor, "I'm happy to serve Lakewood, because eventually I will spend a lot of time there."

In the 1990s, general management and cemetery operations are handled by the president and 24 full-time, year-round office and grounds staff members. The addition of seasonal workers in the summer months brings the workforce to a total of 60. All major decisions are made by committees of the board. The Executive Committee oversees finances, while the Auditing, Building and Grounds, Public Relations, and Nominating Committees manage their respective areas of responsibility.

CHANGES OF TITLE

Though Lakewood's management structure has varied little over the years, job titles have gone through some confusing changes. Paul Anderson's title was changed from Superintendent to Executive Vice President in the early 1970s. After David Hatlestad succeeded Anderson, his job title was changed in 1984, from Executive Vice President to President of the Lakewood Cemetery Associa-

Completed more than 60 years ago, the Lakewood Administration Building receives hundreds of visitors annually. The building's interior, which was renovated in the 1970s, was updated again in 1992.

tion. And President Henry S. Kingman, who had assumed board leadership the year before, became Chairman of the Board of Trustees.

Regardless of their titles, the board's and management's goals remain unchanged. "Today our challenge is to maintain the path of excellence established by our predecessors," says Kingman. As chairman, Kingman works with President Ron Gjerde monitoring projects in progress and overseeing grounds, buildings, and expenditures. Kingman also presides over the annual meeting of the Associates and the Board of Trustees, and chairs the Executive Committee, which oversees the organization's three investment funds: the Permanent Care Fund, the Special Care Fund, and the General Fund.

CARE IN PERPETUITY

When Lakewood was established, lot owners negotiated individually with the Board on annual fees for the care of their lots.

In May 1886, 15 years after Lakewood's founding, the Association first considered starting a fund that would guarantee perpetual maintenance of the cemetery's burial lots. The following year, the Board established the Lakewood Permanent Care Fund, setting aside an initial $25,000 for lot care, maintenance, and improvement. The Lakewood model became a state statute in 1902, requiring Minnesota's 4,000 cemeteries to put aside 20 percent of proceeds from lot sales for cemetery upkeep.

SPECIAL CARE FOREVER

Lakewood's Special Care Fund was created in 1899 by individuals who wanted special services to memorialize friends and loved ones interred at Lakewood. Some contract to have a special memorial flower arrangement placed on a grave to commemorate a birthday or anniversary. Others request flowers on a weekly basis, urn planting and watering, shrub trimming, or monument cleaning. Each contract is individual; costs vary accordingly.

To engage Lakewood's special services, an individual pays a lump sum which is then invested. Half of the investment interest is used to finance the special services; the other half is rolled back into the individual's principal account as a hedge against inflation. Today, Lakewood handles more than 1,800 individual accounts within the Special Care Fund.

Twenty percent of Lakewood's sales proceeds are set aside to guarantee ongoing cemetery maintenance. Families may also pay a special care fee to finance monument cleaning, urn planting, and other services.

Mayor of Minneapolis, U.S. Senator, and Vice President of the United States Hubert H. Humphrey.

HUBERT H. HUMPHREY (1911-1978)

On a bitter cold January day in 1978, more than 3,000 people gathered near Lakewood Cemetery to mourn one of America's great leaders. It was a day of sadness for those attending the funeral of Hubert H. Humphrey, a champion of the people, long known as "the Happy Warrior." But for those at Lakewood Cemetery, it was a triumph of planning, preparation, and cooperation among hundreds of individuals nationwide. ■ Humphrey died on Friday evening, January 13, after a battle with cancer. His remains were flown to Washington, D.C., early the next morning where they lay in state in the Capitol Rotunda, before returning to Minnesota. Although Lakewood President David Hatlestad knew the funeral was to take place at Lakewood, national news announcements informed him that the funeral was sched-

uled for Monday the 16th — less than three days away — not
Wednesday or Thursday as he had thought. There was a staggering
amount of work to do. ■ Once the announcement was made that
Humphrey would be buried at Lakewood, all four telephone lines
were flooded with calls and traffic into the cemetery increased a hun-
dredfold. More than 100 reporters jammed the Lakewood offices in
the next three days. ■ In the meantime, the Humphrey lot was
hastily surveyed and plotted. Reporters, photographers, and network
television and radio crews laden with equipment arrived to stake out
coverage points. ■ The details necessary to ensure security were
endless. President Jimmy Carter, Vice President Walter Mondale, and
scores of national government officials were expected to attend the
graveside services. The Humphrey family wanted to open the services

*Following his death in January 1978, the body of
Hubert H. Humphrey lay in state in the Rotunda of
the Minnesota State Capitol. He was buried in
Lakewood Cemetery on January 16.*

I HAVE ENJOYED MY LIFE,
ITS DISAPPOINTMENTS OUTWEIGHED
BY ITS PLEASURES. I HAVE LOVED MY
COUNTRY IN A WAY THAT SOME
PEOPLE CONSIDER SENTIMENTAL
AND OUT OF STYLE. I STILL DO,
AND I REMAIN AN OPTIMIST,
WITH JOY, WITHOUT APOLOGY,
ABOUT THIS COUNTRY AND
ABOUT THE AMERICAN EXPERIMENT
IN DEMOCRACY.

* HUBERT H. HUMPHREY –
1911-1978

to the public. As a measure of control, press passes were issued to the working press and their technicians, and a press room was set up in the employee lunchroom in the Lakewood Administration Building. ■ Meanwhile, David Hatlestad conferred with the Deputy Chief of Police and the Secret Service to plan the graveside service. They decided that members of the general public could park outside the cemetery and walk to a designated area while a separate area would be roped off for family, national officials, the Honor Guard, and the press. The Secret Service inspected the grounds and the procession route, and ran background checks on all Lakewood employees. Every imaginable security organization was involved in the production. Says Hatlestad: "I had 20 FBI people in my office. We had 200 police cars here." ■ The Director of Minneapolis Civil Defense provided 5,000 feet of rope, auxiliary police for traffic control, a first aid station and a medical team, which treated more than 200 people for frostbite and transported four people to local hospitals. ■ The Lakewood grounds crew pitched in to clear about two feet of snow from five acres of land surrounding the grave site. ■ By 10 a.m. on Monday the 16th, people had started to assemble for the 4 p.m. service — huddling against the sub-zero windchills. Meanwhile, a memorial service was underway at Hope Presbyterian Church in St. Paul. Lakewood monitored the service on radio and television. ■ There were a few last-minute crises to deal with. By 4:17 p.m., the St. Paul service still hadn't finished, and only 45 minutes of daylight remained. A hurried call to the Civil Defense Director brought an emergency generator and floodlights to the cemetery. ■ The procession arrived just after 5 p.m. Among the mourners were the immediate family, Vice President Mondale, about 80 members of Congress, and other dignitaries. Hundreds of pedestrians, who had been watching television and listening to their radios, poured into the cemetery moments before the procession arrived. ■ It was 6:30 p.m. before the casket was lowered and the grave closed, yet some visitors lingered until 8 p.m. ■ In the days that followed, some 200 cars per hour drove through Lakewood to glimpse Humphrey's grave, which stands alone in Lakewood's northeast corner. ■ Humphrey, who began his political career as Mayor

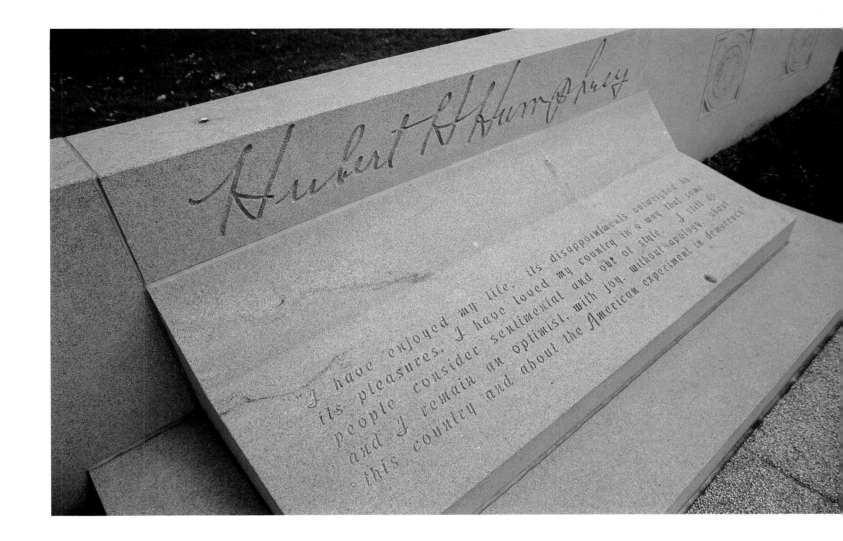

I have enjoyed my life, its disappointments outweighed by its pleasures. I have loved my country in a way that some people consider sentimental and out of style. I still do and I remain an optimist, with joy, without apology, about this country and about the American experiment in democracy.

Hubert H Humphrey

of Minneapolis, was a U.S. Senator from 1948 to 1964, and again from 1970 until his death in 1978. He was Vice President of the United States from 1964 to 1968. ■ Humphrey's signature is etched in stone on the low monument, which was placed at the site later that year. His name is flanked by the state shield, the City of Minneapolis seal, and the seals of the U.S. Senate and vice presidency. ■ People still travel great distances to pay homage to Humphrey. For example, one couple, Solomon and Alyene Slaughter, drove more than 500 miles from Gary, Indiana, in 1981 to visit the grave. Slaughter took three days off from work to make the trip. Once they arrived, he and his wife took turns snapping photos of themselves by the monument. "I appreciate what the man has done for me and for my race...That's the least I could do, if I could come up to show my condolences and re-spect. If I lived in California, I'd still have come," he told a _Minneapolis Tribune_ reporter.

The Humphrey monument, which stands alone in Lakewood's northeast corner, received more than 200 visitors per hour in the days following his funeral. Today, people throughout the United States still visit his grave to pay their respects.

At his death, renowned philanthropist William H. Dunwoody set aside $2 million to establish an industrial trade school to prepare young people for skilled trades. Five years later, in 1918, the Dunwoody Institute was a thriving institution, as it is today, nearly 80 years from its founding.

WILLIAM H. DUNWOODY (1841-1913)

William Hood Dunwoody was a 28-year-old Pennsylvania Quaker with little formal education when he and his wife, Kate, arrived in Minneapolis in 1869. But he did have 10 years of experience in the grain and flour trade. Governor Cadwallader C. Washburn hired him and sent him to Europe to open new markets for Minnesota flour. In 1901, the *Minneapolis Journal* ranked Dunwoody one of 16 millionaires in Minneapolis. ■ Dunwoody's generosity was legendary. In 1911, he pledged $100,000 to the Minneapolis Institute of Arts — at that time, the largest cash gift in the city's history. At his death in 1913, he bequeathed $4.6 million to public and charitable institutions, including $1 million to establish an endowment for The Minneapolis Society of Fine Arts, and $2 million to build and endow the William Hood Dunwoody Industrial Institute to prepare young people for skilled trades.

PLANNED INVESTMENTS

The General Fund holds the bulk of Lakewood's assets. The revenue from lot sales, burials, interment fees, memorials, flowers, and fees for services is deposited into the General Fund, along with the income from investments. Ten percent of crypt sales and 20 percent of lot sales are withheld for the Permanent Care Fund.

Lakewood generates most of its operating revenue from the sale of lots, crypts, and burial niches, and from fees for various services. A small portion of the General Fund investment income supplements the costs of running the cemetery; careful management of expenses minimizes Lakewood's reliance on the fund's capital and maximizes its strong rate of growth.

"The General Fund investment account was established for the purpose of supplementing the Permanent Care Fund in helping to meet our annual operating needs," Gjerde says. "So the investment income from the General Fund acts as a cushion."

TOWARD FINANCIAL SECURITY

Just 20 years after its founding, Lakewood Cemetery was on solid footing and free of debt. The General Fund held $21,000 in 1894; the Permanent Care Fund nearly $38,000.

From that point on, Lakewood's financial growth was uninterrupted. In 1949, after 80 years, Lakewood assets exceeded $4.2 million.

Explosive national growth in the post-World War II era boosted Lakewood's assets to new heights and prepared the Association for the spiraling inflation of the 1970s.

In his 1982 annual report, Superintendent David Hatlestad reviewed how 10 years of inflation had nearly doubled salaries and wages and had pushed operating expenditures toward the $2 million mark.

Yet double-digit inflation also worked to Lakewood's advantage. Sales and income from other revenue-producing activities rose in the 1970s. High interest rates on Lakewood's investments increased its assets.

Lakewood's only major financial setback occurred on "Black Monday," October 19, 1987, when the stock market plunge reduced the value of Lakewood investments by 18.9 percent. Fortunately, the collapse was temporary and today Lakewood enjoys a strong financial position. "Over the years, Lakewood has been

UNLESS YOU MAKE A NOISE, UNLESS YOU MAKE A SOUND, HOW THEY GONNA KNOW THAT YOU'VE EVER BEEN AROUND.
&❧ PEARL ELVERA DAY – 1925-1983

The museum-quality sculpture found in Lakewood Cemetery is enhanced by its lovely natural setting. Visitors who explore the cemetery's grounds are rewarded with a host of beautifully crafted monuments amid spectacular scenery.

blessed with well-managed investment funds," says Russell M. Bennett II, a third-generation trustee. Debt-free, Lakewood manages one of the largest cemetery trust funds in the nation. Investments are carefully managed to retain their purchasing power from one generation to the next.

The growth of Lakewood's assets has prompted changes in money-management strategies over the years. At first the Executive Committee managed the fund exclusively. But in 1890, portions of the fund were turned over to Minneapolis banks: Minneapolis Trust Company, which later consolidated with First National Bank (now First Bank), served as custodian for the Permanent Care Fund for nearly 90 years; Minnesota Loan & Trust, a predecessor of Norwest Bank, managed Lakewood's portfolio of stocks and bonds for more than half a century. In the 1980s, the Board of Trustees transferred the investments from the banks to two investment firms specializing in capital management.

BENEFITING EMPLOYEES

Lakewood adopted a formal plan for employee benefits in 1970. Before that, the Association provided for long-time employees on a case-by-case basis. In 1935, for example, Lakewood gave John Forbes, an employee for more than 50 years, a monthly pension and a lifetime residence at 3537 Hennepin Avenue.

Lakewood has a tradition of treating employees fairly, which has minimized labor problems over the years. Two brief strikes — one in 1937, the other in the 1960s — were both settled amicably. The employees decided to operate without a union as Lakewood's wage scale exceeds union rates and employee safety is a primary concern.

Today, Lakewood's employees enjoy full benefits: health and dental insurance, paid vacations, sick leave, disability insurance, life insurance, and a pension plan. The cost of these benefits equals about 50 percent of the employee's average wage.

FROM FLOWERS TO FINANCE

Lakewood's development has been mirrored in the growth of cemeteries serving other major American cities. In 1887, cemetery managers and administrators throughout the United States created their own professional organization, the American Association of Cemetery Superintendents (AACS).

I CALLED FOR MOTHER,
SHE COULD NOT HEAR ME.
I REACHED FOR HER,
I COULD NOT REACH HER.
    🙚 DAVID E. MUNGER – 1956-1972

The stained glass monument in the Garden of Faith casts brilliant colors in the sunlight.

Superintendent Ralph D. Cleveland, who succeeded A. B. Barton in 1884, represented Lakewood during the first four years of the AACS's existence before stepping aside for incoming Superintendent Arthur W. Hobert. Both men attended the annual AACS convention in cities throughout the United States and exchanged information with other superintendents on issues regarding cemetery management.

Hobert's active participation brought the seventh annual AACS convention to Lakewood in 1893 and again in 1915, when Lakewood set aside $500 to entertain the delegates.

Horticulture and grounds management issues dominated the discussions during the early years of the AACS. In 1888, Cleveland addressed the second annual convention with a talk entitled "Landscape Gardening in Cemeteries." Hobert's lecture topics included "Why New Cemeteries Should Adopt the Lawn Plan" and "What is the Best Way to Get Rid of Gophers?" At their conventions, members debated these and other topics such as the benefits of various grass seed, shrubbery, and flower planting.

Over a century old, the AACS is now the American Cemetery Association (ACA), a professional organization attuned to modern problems. Sales, marketing, and similar business issues have joined landscaping and beautification as the focus of cemetery management. Today, Lakewood and its President, Ron Gjerde, take an active role in the ACA as well as in state and metropolitan-area associations.

THE TIMES ARE A-CHANGING

In 1899, Charles Loring addressed the AACS in New Haven, Connecticut: "The greatest curse that I find in regard to the cemeteries of the United States is that...the majority of them are run for profit. A cemetery should be the people's sacred spot; every dollar that is put into it should be...for the benefit of those who have to lay their loved ones there."

While Lakewood has maintained the vision of a non-profit organization, many other cemeteries have not. By the 1980s, the merger and acquisition fever sweeping corporate America had infiltrated the funeral industry. Profit-seeking conglomerates offered a full line of services, including funeral homes, cemeteries, and cremations.

GETTING THE WORD OUT

Changes are definitely taking place in the industry and Lakewood is adapting. Yet Lakewood's first marketing venture began more than a half-century ago, when Robert L. Brooks, Sr., Lyndon King, and Angus Morrison formed the Public Relations Committee to promote the cemetery in Minneapolis. With an initial budget of $7,500, the committee contracted with an "outstanding advertising man" to produce Lakewood's first newspaper ads.

Over the years, a steadily growing budget has brought increasingly sophisticated communications to Lakewood's intended audience. Newspaper ads have been supplemented with full-page inserts, booklets, and color brochures. Billboards have been used to get the message out, and in the 1980s, Lakewood expanded into video communications, creating television commercials and audio-visual programs to attract customers.

BEFORE THE NEED ARISES

In 1951, in response to competitive changes in the industry, Lakewood launched a "pre-need" sales program. While Lakewood and other cemeteries had previously sold products and services to the bereaved after a person's death, many American cemeteries took the initiative and actively pursued sales before death occurred. Some cemeteries employed dozens of salespeople who aggressively competed for business using this pre-need strategy.

To meet the challenge, Lakewood hired independent sales consultant E. C. Leonard to develop a sales program. While Lakewood's full-time staff continued to handle sales in the traditional manner, Leonard and his team, working on a commission basis, successfully developed Lakewood's pre-need business. Then, in 1964, the Association initiated plans for the new mausoleum and columbarium and the Board decided to restructure Lakewood's sales operations into a three-member staff that handles all sales, including walk-in, call-in, and pre-need. Today, their basic sales philosophy closely follows Lakewood's traditional style. The three full-time sales counselors take a low-key approach and avoid the high-pressure tactics of many cemetery organizations. Like other employees, the sales counselors have a long history with Lakewood.

Lakewood's timely participation in the new pre-need strategy kept pace with changes sweeping the industry. Before 1960, people in the prime of life rarely

Many of Lakewood's monuments inspire hope and quiet reflection.

shopped for burial lots. But since then, pre-need sales have increased rapidly — from 10 percent in the 1960s to 20 percent in the 1970s. Today, 50 percent of cemetery and funeral sales are pre-need, and pre-need sales account for 80 percent of revenues.

NEW VENUES

Lakewood has expanded its sales, marketing, and promotion efforts into other areas as well. In 1975, Lakewood participated in seminars on death and dying at the University of Minnesota. It sought customers' feedback through surveys designed to determine needs, attitudes, and potential problems. It sponsored flower shows at Christmas, Easter, and Memorial Day, drawing 500 visitors at each event. It conducted tours of the grounds and the chapel, a service that continues today for Lakewood's more than 120,000 yearly visitors.

Lakewood's competitive position was also enhanced by broadening its burial options and services. Once Lakewood offered only traditional lot burial. By 1967, the cemetery was providing a variety of single and multiple interment options, including mausoleum crypts, garden crypts, lawn crypts, columbarium niches, and cremorial gardens.

Lakewood's marketing and development efforts have been successful. From its founding, Lakewood has been the leading cemetery in the area, and by 1975, it was handling 37 percent of dispositions in the Minneapolis metropolitan area.

AN EMERGING TREND

Cremation is becoming a popular alternative to traditional burial throughout the world. Cremation accounts for 80 percent of the dispositions in Japan, 70 percent in Britain, and 16 percent in the United States. Analysts say that the ratio of cremations to burials is rising at about one percent a year in the United States, with higher rates on the West Coast and in metropolitan areas. Some experts predict that cremation will account for 30 percent of the dispositions in America by 1995. Minnesota reflects the national trend — cremation accounts for about 25 percent of Hennepin County's dispositions.

Increasing family mobility, scarcity of land, and the high cost of traditional funerals have contributed to the rising popularity of cremation.

The stained glass walls of the Lakewood Community Mausoleum and Columbarium are tributes to personal beliefs and spirituality.

To meet the challenge of decreasing traditional burials, Lakewood has expanded its burial options and emphasizes the importance of memorialization. As a result, the cremated remains of many individuals are placed in the Lakewood columbarium, the cremorial garden, or traditional lots. "Cremated remains are just as sacred as the body itself," says William King, great-grandson of Lakewood founder William King, and a trustee until 1990.

Trustee Henry Doerr's view is representative of a changing concept of memorialization. "We consider our family plot a memorial rather than a burial lot. My mother's body was donated to medical research, but we have a headstone for her. My son's body was cremated and his cremated remains were spread on a ski trail named for him in Montana. But we memorialize him here."

LIMITATIONS AND OPPORTUNITIES

In 1972, the Association took a significant step toward prolonging Lakewood's development by reclaiming unused burial lots. Most of those lots, purchased in the 1870s and 1880s, were returned to inventory and offered to the public.

"I'd estimate that we have about 35 acres of undeveloped land," says Ron Gjerde. "If we used that land for traditional grave spaces, we'd have enough for about 36,000 burials."

In 1990, Lakewood established a new record by handling more than 2,000 services, 1,000 of which involved burial in traditional lots. By 1991, Lakewood had handled 119,000 burials and 27,000 cremations, for a total of 146,000 interments.

Even at this rate, Lakewood can continue to serve well into the 21st century. Ron Gjerde is predicting space availability for at least another 50 to 60 years, with burials continuing well beyond the time when all lots have been purchased. His predictions are based on the public's demand for alternative burial options and on Lakewood's desire to maximize its use of space. Anticipating the future, Gjerde and the Board continually evaluate how best to allocate Lakewood's resources and best serve public needs. "Buying a cemetery lot is one of the least expensive investments you'll ever make," says David Hatlestad. "Because there are no taxes and no assessments, you pay one price and it's maintained for the rest of time."

THE GREATEST OF THESE IS LOVE...
GOD LOVES YOU, AND I LOVE YOU.
❧ GREGORY THOMAS DAY – 1955-1982

Indeed, Lakewood's trustees and managers from its very beginning have set their sights on the rest of time. The buildings and other physical structures will eventually need renovation and replacement. Trees that are now seedlings will someday tower over buildings, but their lifespans will also end. The rolls of people interred at Lakewood, now in computer files, will be transferred to new systems with each generation of technology's advance. But even when every lot at Lakewood is occupied, every crypt filled, and every niche in the columbarium taken, the care and maintenance of this beautiful haven will continue. At Lakewood, today's decisions are made not only for tomorrow and next year, but also for perpetuity.

The corridors and alcoves of the Lakewood Community Mausoleum and Columbarium are designed for crypt interment. Individual names and dates of birth and death appear on each crypt's marble face.

Even though it reached its centennial mark more than 20 years ago, Lakewood Cemetery officials predict that space will be available for at least 50 to 60 years. Beyond that, sound financial planning has ensured that the beauty and serenity found at Lakewood will endure in perpetuity.

TRUSTEES

Lakewood Cemetery is governed by a nine-member Board of Trustees.
The Trustees are appointed to "seats," which they hold until age 70.
The Trustees of Lakewood, listed by seat, have included:

Officers

PRESIDENT

Calvin G. Goodrich	1871-1874
Charles M. Loring	1874-1877
George A. Brackett	1877
Dorilus Morrison	1877-1879, 1882-1889
Hugh G. Harrison	1879-1882
George Pillsbury	1888-1898
W. D. Washburn	1898-1912
George Brackett	1912-1921
C. S. Langdon	1921-1941
Perry Harrison	1941-1948
Robert L. Brooks, Sr.	1948-1974
John P. Snyder, Jr.	1974-1983
David C. Hatlestad	1983-1989
Ronald A. Gjerde, Jr.	1989-present

VICE PRESIDENT

R. J. Mendenhall	1898-1906
George A. Brackett	1906-1912
Calvin G. Goodrich	1912-1915
C. S. Langdon	1916-1921
Perry Harrison	1921-1941
Robert L. Brooks, Sr.	1941-1948
Thomas Harrison	1948-1974
Goodrich Lowry	1974-1975
Henry S. Kingman, Jr.	1975-1983
Ronald A. Gjerde, Jr.	1983-1989

TREASURER

R. J. Mendenhall	1871-1877
Charles M. Loring	1877-1906
W. D. Hale	1906-1915
C. S. Langdon	1915-1941
Perry Harrison	1941-1945
Justus F. Lowe (investment counselor, non-trustee)	1945-1963
Benton Case	1963-1974
Richard Vaughan	1974-1976
Clinton Morrison	1976-1987
E. Peter Gillette, Jr.	1987-present

SECRETARY

(Prior to 1920 the superintendent performed secretary's job)

John R. Vanderlip	1920-1935
Lyndon King	1935-1951
Laurence Eggleston	1951-1966
Goodrich Lowry	1966-1974
Russell M. Bennett II	1974-1983
John S. Pillsbury, Jr.	1983-1984
C. Angus Wurtele	1984-present

Beginning at the annual meeting 12/14/83:

    Chairman – Henry S. Kingman, Jr.

    Vice Chairman – Russell M. Bennett II

Lakewood also has a Board of Associates. Associate members have included:

BOARD OF ASSOCIATES

Dorilus Morrison	1871-1897
Calvin G. Goodrich	1871-1893
William S. King	1871-1900
A. B. Barton	1871-1905
Thomas Lowry	1871-1909
George A. Brackett	1871-1921
William D. Washburn	1871-1912
William P. Westfall	1871-1893
Robert Brace Langdon	1871-1895
Richard J. Mendenhall	1871-1906
Hugh G. Harrison	1871-1893
Paris Gibson	1871-1893
Levi Butler	1871-1893
A. Tyler	1871-1893
Samuel C. Gale	1871-1916
George Pillsbury	1893-1898
Charles M. Loring	1893-1922
L. P. Hubbard	1893-1909
Samuel Hill	1893-1905
Calvin G. Goodrich, Jr.	1893-1915
Loren Fletcher	1893-1919
Cavour S. Langdon	1895-1944

Clinton Morrison	1898-1913	George D. Dayton II	1964-1979
Gregor Menzel	1898-1906	Richard Vaughn	1967-1979
W. D. Hale	1901-1915	Russell M. Bennett II	1969-present
Chapin R. Brackett	1905-1944	Stephen P. Duffy, Jr.	1973-present
W. D. Washburn, Jr.	1905-1930	John S. Pillsbury III	1974-1981
A. C. Loring	1906-1932	Ruth Leslie Bean	1975-1980
George H. Partridge	1906-1932	Jane West	1976-present
Horace Lowry	1909-1931	C. Angus Wurtele	1976-present
Walter A. Eggleston	1909-1936	Margaret Ankeny	1979-present
John R. Vanderlip	1912-1935	E. Peter Gillette, Jr.	1979-present
F. B. Snyder	1913-1951	David T. Bennett	1981-present
Perry Harrison	1915-1950	David C. Hatlestad	1981-1989
Donald Goodrich	1916-1951	James W. Nelson	1983-present
E. C. Gale	1916-1943	Glenn S. Brooks	1985-1988
Alfred Pillsbury	1919-1950	Helen S. Johnson	1985-present
Lyndon King	1925-1963	David P. Crosby	1985-present
Angus W. Morrison	1925-1949	Edward (Ned) Dayton	1988-present
*Robert L. Brooks, Sr.	1930-1974	Henry Doerr	1988-present
Russell H. Bennett	1931-1976	Christine A. Morrison	1989-present
Thomas G. Harrison	1932-1975	Ronald A. Gjerde, Jr.	1991-present
Albert H. Crosby	1933-1945		
Laurence A. Eggleston	1936-1969	**SUPERINTENDENTS**	
John P. Snyder, Sr.	1936-1959	A. B. Barton	1872-1884
Richard Gale	1943-1967	Ralph Cleveland	1884-1891
Goodrich Lowry	1945-1983	A. W. Hobert	1891-1920
John S. Pillsbury, Jr.	1945-1984	Arthur Nuessle	1920-1946
W. Hubert Kennedy	1947-1971	Paul W. Anderson	1946-1972
Clinton Morrison	1949-1987	David C. Hatlestad	1972-1983
John deLaittre	1950-1962		
Henry Crosby	1950-1953		
Wilkes Covey	1951-1960		
Benton Case	1951-1976		
**John P. Snyder, Jr.	1953-1985		
William A. King	1959-1990		
Robert L. Brooks, Jr.	1960-1985		
Henry S. Kingman, Jr.	1962-present		

* Served as Honorary Chairman from 1974 until his death in 1989.

** Served as Chairman Emeritus from 1985 until his death in 1989.

Photo Credits

MINNESOTA HISTORICAL SOCIETY

Page 9: Fjelde Family at Claudine and Henrik Fjelde Monument, Lakewood Cemetery, 1890's. **Page 16:** Caskets in Lakewood Crematory Room in 1920, *Minneapolis Journal.* **Page 20:** Minneapolis in 1857, B. F. Upton. **Page 21:** Indian Tepees at Bridge Square, Minneapolis, 1854, from original daguerreotype. **Page 22:** St. Anthony Falls and East Side Mills, 1867. **Page 23:** The Nicollet House, 1890, Jacoby. **Page 24:** Lakewood Cemetery, 1890's, Lakewood Archives. **Page 29:** William S. King. **Page 30:** Lyndale Hotel, Minneapolis, 1880. **Page 31:** Thomas Lowry's home (later home of T. B. Walker), Minneapolis, 1905, Seet. **Page 33:** Hose Co. 1 answering a fire alarm, 1907, *Minneapolis Journal.* **Page 34:** Honorable W. D. Washburn. **Page 35:** Northwestern National Bank, Minneapolis, 1875, Illingworth. **Page 37:** Washington Ave., 1873. **Page 38:** Mendenhall Greenhouse, Minneapolis, 1890. **Page 39:** Charles M. Loring, Rugg. **Page 40:** Pond in Loring Park, Minneapolis, 1890. **Page 41:** Pence Opera House, Minneapolis, 1869. **Page 42:** Dakota Tribe, 1875. **Page 43:** Samuel Wm. Pond, Rev. Gideon Hollister Pond. **Page 45:** Calhoun Boulevard at 36th St., Minneapolis, 1905. **Page 50:** Minneapolis Symphony Orchestra, Emil Oberhoffer conducting, 1910. **Page 64:** Lake Harriet, Minneapolis, 1895, F. E. Haynes. **Page 65:** Old style horse-drawn hearse, 1905. **Page 66:** Decoration Day Parade in Minneapolis, 1924. **Page 67:** Chapel, Lakewood Cemetery, Aug. 13, 1948, *Minneapolis Star Journal.* **Page 69:** Mrs. Brown at Lakewood Cemetery, 1900, Guy M. Baltuff. **Page 70:** Floyd B. Olson's grave, Lakewood Cemetery, 1936. **Page 94:** Old Cemetery Office, Lakewood Cemetery, 1903, Sweet. **Page 96:** Lakewood Cemetery, 1903. **Page 100:** Superintendent's Cottage, Lakewood Cemetery, Minneapolis, 1920. **Page 113:** Daughters of the American Revolution Procession at Leamington Hotel, Minneapolis, Sept. 27, 1923. **Page 120:** Hubert H. Humphrey. **Page 121:** Hubert H. Humphrey lying in state, Minnesota State Capitol Rotunda. **Page 124:** In training for the Navy at Dunwoody Institute, 1918.

LAKEWOOD CEMETERY ARCHIVES

Page 13: George H. Knowlton deed. **Page 27:** Tombstones. **Page 53:** Easter flowers. **Page 68:** Casket surrounded by flowers in chapel. **Page 71:** Floyd B. Olson funeral. **Pages 72, 73:** Lakewood Cemetery. **Pages 97, 98:** Lakewood Cemetery office. **Page 101:** Lakewood Chapel. **Page 112:** Mausoleum construction.

PAUL AARSTAD

Page 54: Lakewood Cemetery's greenhouse.

PER BREIEHAGEN

Page 7: Kingman. **Page 11:** Pillsbury monument. **Page 15:** Angel. **Page 17:** Lawn crypt. **Page 19:** Walker monument. **Page 26:** Menzel monument. **Page 28:** Mill explosion monument. **Page 46:** Winter wildlife. **Page 47:** Lake. **Page 49:** 36th Street flower bed. **Page 55:** Tulips. **Page 56:** Flower bed. **Page 57:** Francis monument. **Page 58:** Flower bed. **Page 59:** Tulips at lake. **Page 60:** Cemetery. **Page 61:** Winter scene. **Page 74:** Hankenson monument. **Page 75:** Pagoda. **Page 77:** Angel. **Page 78:** Stone monument. **Page 79:** Lawrence monument. **Page 80:** Civil War cannon. **Page 82:** Nelson monument. **Page 83:** Statue. **Page 84:** Lowry-Goodrich mausoleum. **Page 85:** deVillier monument. **Page 86:** Wood Mausoleum. **Page 87:** Architectural detail. **Page 88:** MFD Relief Assoc. monument. **Page 89:** Elk's Rest. **Page 90:** Rocheleau monument. **Page 91:** Garden of Faith. **Page 92:** Obelisk. **Page 93:** Fridley monument. **Page 115:** Stained glass windows of mausoleum. (below) Detail of glass. **Page 116:** Board of Trustees. **Page 118:** Administration Building. **Page 123:** Hubert H. Humphrey monument. **Page 126:** Women and child monument. **Page 128:** Garden of Faith stained glass detail. **Page 129:** Statue of woman. **Page 130:** Stained glass wall. **Page 132:** Alcove in Mausoleum.

PHILIP PROWSE

Page 102: Chapel doors. **Page 105:** Chapel interior.

MITCH KEZAR

Cover: Monument. **Pages 8, 10, 12, 18, 44, 52, 63, 117, 133:** Fall scenery. **Page 119:** Grave marker.

CARMICHAEL LYNCH ADVERTISING

Page 6: Fountain. **Page 104:** Chapel dome. **Page 106:** Chapel interior. **Page 108:** Angels circling chapel dome. **Page 111:** Love, Faith, Memory, and Hope. **Page 114:** Pool of Reflections.

Acknowledgments

The Trustees of Lakewood Cemetery wish to thank the many individuals and organizations who provided information and photographs for this book. Special thanks are due to photographers Mitch Kezar, Phil Prowse, and Per Breiehagen, and to the Minnesota Historical Society, the Hennepin County Historical Society, and the *Minneapolis Star Tribune* for their assistance; and to the following individuals who provided written information and personal recollections:

Paul Aarestad

Paul W. Anderson

Russell M. Bennett II

Henry Doerr

John Erwin

E. Peter Gillette, Jr.

Ronald A. Gjerde, Jr.

David C. Hatlestad

Lee Hilary

Jim Jansen

William King

Henry S. Kingman, Jr.

Mary Lerman

Lance M. Neckar

Wallace E. Nelson

Gayle Olson

Jim Ostvig

Bernard S. Paulson

John S. Pillsbury, Jr.

Donald Strickland

John L. Werness

Index

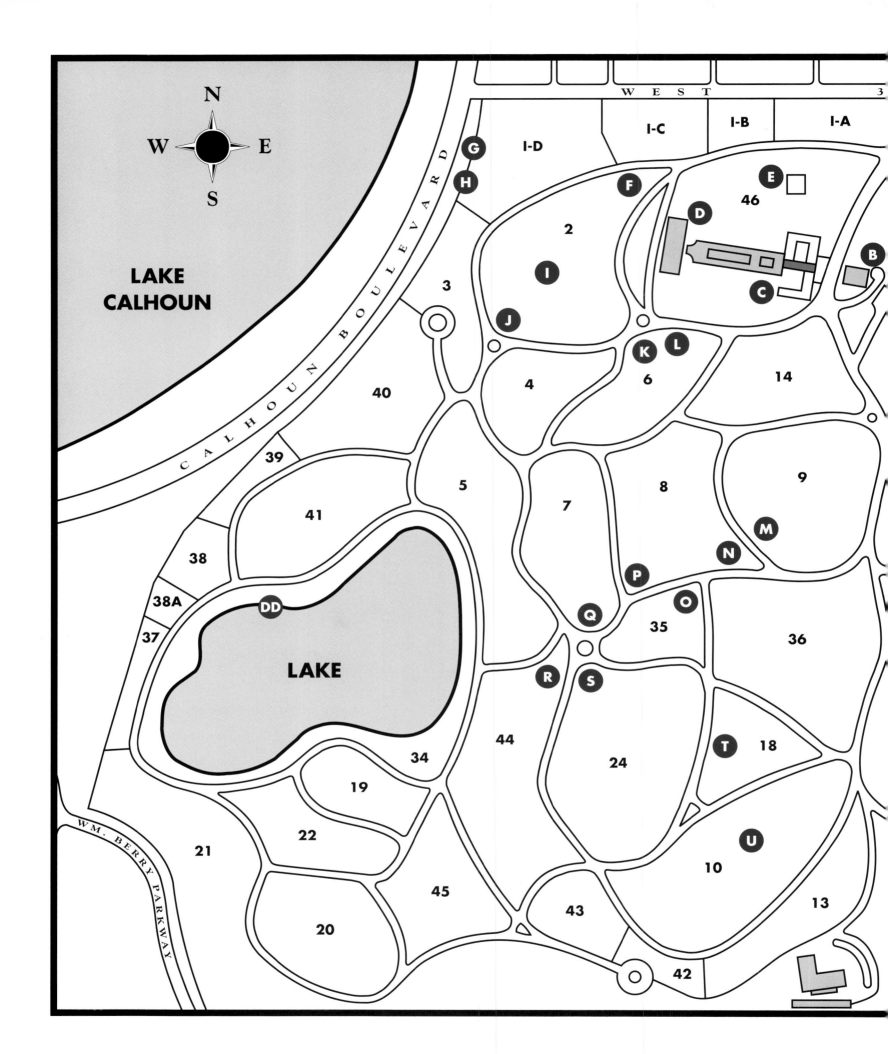

LAKE CALHOUN

CALHOUN BOULEVARD

WEST

I-A

I-B

I-C

I-D

G

H

F

E

46

D

B

C

2

I

3

J

K

L

4

6

14

40

39

5

7

8

9

41

M

38

N

38A

DD

P

37

O

Q

35

36

LAKE

R

S

44

T

18

34

24

19

U

22

10

21

45

13

20

43

42

W. M. BERRY PARKWAY

N

W   E

S

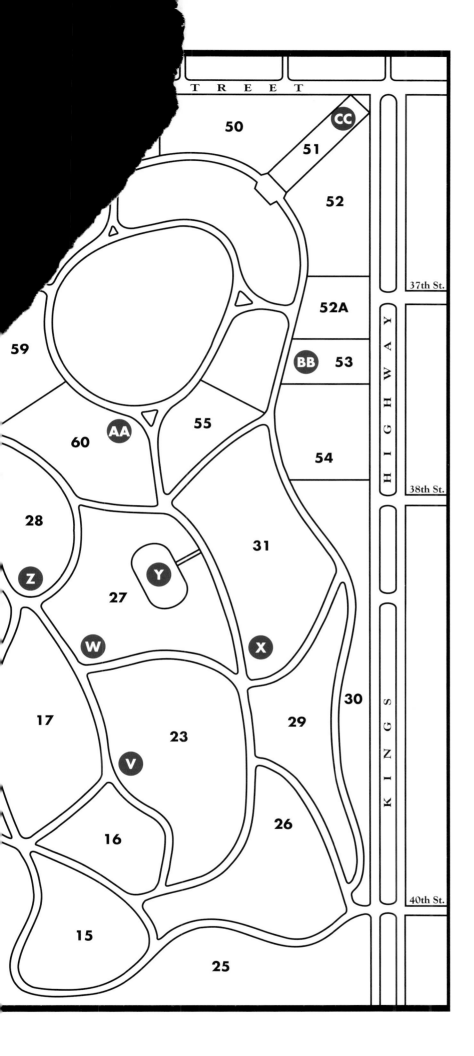

POINTS OF INTEREST

A	Administration Building
B	Lakewood Chapel
C	Lawn and Garden Crypts
D	Lakewood Memorial Mausoleum
E	T. B. Walker Monument
F	Fridley Monument
G	Sir Joseph Francis Monument
H	Flour Mill Explosion Monument
I	Pillsbury Monument
J	Maggie Menzel Monument
K	Mary Stevens Monument
L	Charles M. Loring Monument
M	Minneapolis Fire Department Monument
N	Grand Army of the Republic Monument
O	St. Mary's Greek Orthodox Church
P	International Order of Odd Fellows
Q	Elk's Rest
R	Emil Oberhoffer Monument
S	Soldiers' Monument
T	Governor Floyd Olson Monument
U	William H. Dunwoody Monument
V	Rocheleau Monument
W	Lowry-Goodrich Mausoleum
X	William Henry Eustis Monument
Y	Garden of Memories Sun Dial
Z	Showman's Rest
AA	Praying Hands Monument
BB	Negative Relief Carving of Christ
CC	Senator Hubert H. Humphrey Monument
DD	Indian Treaty Line of 1805